To my friends at the
United Methodist
Church in
Wilsonville.

The Lord bless you,
Jeanette Chaffee

ACCLAIM FOR JEANETTE CHAFFEE AND *EXTRAVAGANT GRACES*

"Are you facing a crisis in your marriage? Your family? Your career? Even your faith? You are not alone—there are others who have experienced these things. And they also encountered God's faithfulness in the midst of their difficult circumstances. *Extravagant Graces* is full of stories that will inspire and encourage."

JIM DALY, president of Focus on the Family

"*Extravagant Graces* is a must-read. We have all dealt with difficulties in life. This book captures the power of how God uses those difficulties to shape and guide our lives. You will be encouraged and challenged by the personal stories."

LES STECKEL, president and CEO of Fellowship of Christian Athletes, NFL coach twenty-three years (twice to the Super Bowl), head coach of the Minnesota Vikings, San Francisco 49ers player, Golden Gloves boxing champion

"Jeanette Chaffee is simply another example that God uses ordinary people in extraordinary ways."

RICHARD STEARNS, president of World Vision U.S. and author of *Unfinished: Believing is Only the Beginning*

"Exciting… inspirational. Praise the Lord for Jeanette's life and testimony."

PAT BOONE, actor, singer, songwriter

“I know *Extravagant Graces* will be a blessing. May God richly bless you, keep you, and use you for the glory of His Name, Jeanette. It is wonderful to know of the Lord's marvelous protection of your life in the plane accident. We do rejoice with you.**”**

CLIFF BARROWS, team member
and music program director of Billy
Graham Evangelistic Association

“I had the pleasure of interviewing Jeanette Chaffee during her visit to *The 700 Club*. She shared her harrowing experience on the TWA 840 bombing in a clear, lucid manner. She was an effective eyewitness to a real-life drama. She was an asset to the program that day.**”**

BEN KINCHLOW, former host of *The 700 Club*

“Jeanette Chaffee is a living testimony that God has a perfect, profound and extravagant destiny for each of us.**”**

BILL DOLAN, president / creative
director of Spirit Media

“I am delighted to encourage a wide distribution of this amazing collection of unique, unpublished first-hand stories, photos, and quotes from valued Christian personalities. This beautiful book is heartwarming, encouraging and informative. It reflects Jeanette's zeal and enthusiasm for helping others develop an authentic relationship with Christ. You will treasure your personal copy and find it a valued gift for others.**”**

BOBBIE HASSMAN, author,
president of Panache Living for Women

"If you are looking for inspiring stories of some of God's choice people, *Extravagant Graces* is for you. If you want to see how the Lord has used available men and women in remarkable, eternity-changing ways, *Extravagant Graces* is for you. If you are ready to be challenged to a deeper walk with the Lord Jesus Christ, *Extravagant Graces* is for you."

STEVE RAY, senior editor and research coordinator of English Language Institute/China

"I encourage you to experience a cup of cold water for your soul through these timely and timeless words. Real life, real hope, from the real Jesus. Enjoy."

ALAN HLAVKA, lead pastor of Good Shepherd Community Church, Family Life Marriage conference speaker

"When reading about the lives of well-known Christians, our response can be to envy God's work in them and wonder why God doesn't seem to work that way in ours. But the real-life stories in *Extravagant Graces* wonderfully inspire us to reflect on how God uses each one of us in our own unique settings to glorify Himself and further His kingdom purposes."

KATHY J. (SAINT) DROWN, daughter of martyred missionary, Nate Saint, and cofounder of Truths for Living

"Riveting. The people Jeanette cameos are so famous one would think there's nothing to be learned. She uncovers brand-new information which is not common knowledge or previously published."

LYNN SAINT, family member of Nate Saint

"We feel that Jeanette would be an asset to any congregation or other group of people. We know that God will allow her to minister to those in need by hearing her special story."

DAVID ALDRICH, former producer
of *The Gary Randall Show*

"Behind every great story of success and impact for the kingdom of God is usually an equally powerful story of overcoming pain and obstacles. One of the most difficult and inevitable lessons we learn is that God often uses the crucible of this life to strengthen and deepen us into the type of men and women that reflect Him in a broken world. In *Extravagant Graces*, Jeanette very brilliantly unfolds the stories of a few of these people who have had a great impact on our world, and shows how they have experienced extravagant grace to overcome and live the life of faith."

TONY OVERSTAKE, University of Oregon
Ducks athletic chaplain, U of O Fellowship
of Christian Athletes campus director

"Welcome to a grace-filled, marvelous book where God's extravagance walks off the pages. How long has it been since you've read a book that inspires you to want to change your world?"

CAROL URBEN, executive assistant

"*Extravagant Graces* shows God's faithfulness through fascinating personal life experiences of people who have walked close to God. I was challenged, inspired and encouraged in my spiritual journey. You will be too."

DAVID ABUBANAT, regional
ministry leader of Pioneers

"God has given Jeanette a great speaking ability which she has chosen to use to share the Gospel with others. What a privilege to spend time with a woman whose joyous personality reflects the love of Jesus. Jeanette has really touched our hearts as well as others, and many to come."

NATHAN DIGESARE, former
coproducer of Dino Ministries

"*Extravagant Graces* highlights God's amazing love and redemptive work captured in real life stories. The midair TWA bomb explosion is a remarkable example of God's sovereignty, as Jeanette lived to share her story and the vital importance of making peace with God before the unexpected literally erupts. Her frightening experience, as well as interviews with remarkable men and women of faith, are the powerful seeds God used to grow *Extravagant Graces*."

LINDA J. BRADLEY, board member
of Illustra Media Productions

"Jeanette Chaffee was the guest speaker at our Sunday service. People were deeply moved by her sharing. She was an excellent communicator. I commend her very highly to you as a deeply committed Christian with a vital message to share."

REV. TOM WILSON, former pastor of First
Church of the Nazarene (Salem, Oregon)

"*Extravagant Graces* is readable and brings refreshment to a parched heart. It's one of the year's most compelling books."

RENEE SCOTT, assistant to a college president

To Mom and Dad

**Your faithful prayers for me
every single day of my life
are extravagant blessings**

EXTRAVAGANT GRACES

23 INSPIRING STORIES OF FACING IMPOSSIBLE ODDS

JEANETTE CHAFFEE

EXTRAVAGANT GRACES CREDITS

Holy Bible **translations used:** *King James, New King James, Living Bible, New International Version, New American Standard Bible*

"We Rest on Thee" hymn by Edith G. Cherry ©1895 (public domain)

"Finlandia" hymn by Jean Sibelius ©1899 (public domain)

"The Plan of the Master Weaver" poem (author unknown)

"When You Thought I Wasn't Looking" poem (author unknown)

Untitled poem by Joyce Bruemmer Hulstedt (used with permission)

Photos courtesy of Robert Surcouf, Jeanette Chaffee (by Cahill Studios), Donnie Dee, Stephen Arterburn, Evelyn Saint Jimenez, Lynn Saint, David Saint, Martha Saint Berberian, Shannon Richardson, Steve Richardson, Paul Richardson, Valerie Powers, Don Richardson, Ken Medema, Marilee Pierce Dunker, Valerie Shepard, Christiana R.S. Greene, Phyliss Masters (©2014 by Phyliss Masters), Bill and Nancie Carmichael, Sandra Aldrich (by Monarch Digital), Anne Graham Lotz (by Russ Busby), John D. Wilson, Wesley Dale (©2014 by Stan Dale family), David Martin (©2014 by David Martin), Paul Newman, and Marc Zeedar.

Shirley Dobson's original article *Where God Guides ... God Provides* and photo are used with permission. She retains all other rights to their use, now and in perpetuity.

Book cover and interior design by Marc Zeedar (DesignWrite.com).

WestBow Press books may be ordered through booksellers or by contacting:

WestBow Press
A Division of Thomas Nelson & Zondervan
1663 Liberty Drive
Bloomington, IN 47403
www.westbowpress.com
1 (866) 928-1240

ISBN: 978-1-4908-2976-0 (sc)
ISBN: 978-1-4908-2978-4 (hc)

Library of Congress Control Number: 2014914489

Printed in the United States of America.

WestBow Press rev. date: 8/14/2014

I am with you; that is all you need.

My power shows up best in weak people.

God

2 Corinthians 12:9

EX-TRAV-A-GANT

lavish, extremely opulent,
fabulous, costly

❧ CONTENTS ❧

Introduction
Twenty-three stories, one theme **19**

JEANETTE CHAFFEE
Terror in the Sky
Suspended midair between life and death **22**

DON & CAROL RICHARDSON
Behind the Peace Child
Canoeing with a baby through crocodile-infested
waters to live with cannibals **33**

DAVID STOOP
A Different Kind of Father
Living in denial, a man wants to be the father he never had **40**

STEPHEN ARTERBURN
From Depression to Wholeness
A suicidal overeater becomes an inspirational
speaker heard by millions **45**

EVELYN SAINT JIMENEZ & OLIVE FLEMING LIEFELD

Speared: Betrayed by New Friends
They came in peace... **51**

Cloud of Witnesses
Discovering secrets thirty years after
her husband's murder **73**

ELISABETH ELLIOT & VALERIE ELLIOT SHEPARD

You've Gone Too Far This Time, God
Isolated in the Amazon jungle with a
three-year-old daughter **81**

Survive? Impossible!
Widowed with an infant, how could she go on living? **83**

My Mother's Heartaches and Joys
Wasn't it bad enough having her first husband die? **85**

KEN MEDEMA

A Different Way of Seeing
Born blind, yet he performs before presidents **98**

SHIRLEY DOBSON

Where God Guides ... God Provides
What good could possibly come from leaving
their beloved home of thirty years? **103**

DONNIE DEE

Journey From a Broken Home to the NFL
After living with an alcoholic gold medalist, this
NFL player gets a new boss **107**

MARILEE PIERCE DUNKER

Finishing Well
The four-year-old girl is asked to sing before thousands **117**

JERRY & SUSANNE MCCLAIN

Not Always Happy Days
Overnight, a Hollywood couple goes from
having it all to losing it all **121**

BILL & NANCIE CARMICHAEL

Scary Times
When a dad breaks his legs and an arm,
can his family survive? **131**

Not the Daughter of Their Dreams
They longed for a daughter—they got Amy **133**

SANDRA ALDRICH

Unprepared
Getting married, she never imagines death **139**

I Choose Joy
A unique way to cope with breast cancer **142**

ANNE GRAHAM LOTZ

A Sense of Loss … a Sense of Gain
A loving daughter and father are forced apart **145**

EDITH SCHAEFFER

Reflections of Death and Heaven
A dying man's last words to his sweetheart **155**

Planned by Accident
An inquisitive visitor begins a trend **158**

PHYLISS MASTERS

Murdered by Lords of the Earth
Turning tragedy into triumph **163**

DINO KARTSONAKIS

Small Problems
What is key to a world-class pianist? **190**

PART 2 MORE EXTRAVAGANT GRACES

Tributes
You've just read their public stories…
Now hear what their families have to say **195**

SANDRA ALDRICH

A Woman of Faith **195**
by Holly Hulen, daughter

…And Another Life Lesson **198**
by Jay Aldrich, son

BILL & NANCIE CARMICHAEL

Rooted in Grace **199**
by Christian Carmichael, son

Loving in Spite of Differences **201**
by Amy Carmichael Caviggia, adopted daughter

JEANETTE CHAFFEE

Unforgettable **202**
by Monica Plata, niece

DONNIE DEE

My Obedient Servant Leader **204**
by Johnny Dee, son

ELISABETH ELLIOT

A Regal Lady **207**
by Christiana R.S. Greene, third grandchild

My Irreplaceable Namesake **209**
by Elisabeth S. Martin, second grandchild

VALERIE ELLIOT SHEPARD

To My Lovely Mama **210**
by Christiana R.S. Greene, daughter

PHYLISS MASTERS

Home **212**
by Crissie Masters Rask, daughter

JERRY & SUSANNE MCCLAIN

God's Restorative Grace **215**
by Jarret McClain, son

DON & CAROL RICHARDSON

Stargazing With Dad **219**
by Shannon Richardson, second son

On Top of the World **220**
by Valerie Richardson Powers, daughter

Saving Me From Carl **222**
by Shannon Richardson, second son

Extravagant Quotes **226**

An Extravagant Invitation **233**

Acknowledgments **234**

About the Author **235**

"THE PLAN OF THE MASTER WEAVER"

My Life is but a weaving
between my Lord and me;
I cannot choose the colors
He worketh steadily.

Oft times He weaveth sorrow
And I, in foolish pride,
Forget He sees the upper,
And I the under side.

Not til the loom is silent
And the shuttles cease to fly,
Shall God unroll the canvas
And explain the reason why.

The dark threads are as needful
In the Weaver's skillful hand,
As the threads of gold and silver
In the pattern He has planned.

He knows, He loves, He cares,
Nothing this truth can dim,
He gives His very best to those
Who leave the choice with Him.

Author Unknown

When God is going to do
something wonderful,
He always starts
with a hardship;

When God is going to do
something amazing, He
starts with an impossibility.

Anne Lamott

Introduction

Twenty-three stories, one theme

BY JEANETTE CHAFFEE

WENDY TOLD ME: "THESE STORIES ARE AMAZING! YOU'VE *got* to put them in a book." My response was skeptical. I've been interviewing influential people for more than thirty years, but without plans to put them in a book.

I prayed and felt my friend was right. I hauled out dozens of cassette tapes, CDs, and storage boxes of transcriptions. As I studied the interviews, I discovered that, though I hadn't chosen any particular topic, the Master Author had. All of them faced impossible situations, including my own experience with terrorism. The theme became clear: *What's one of the most difficult experiences you've faced and how did God help you survive?*

Inspired, I began working this material into stories and conducting fresh interviews. I was continually struck with God's calming presence in horrific situations. What an incredible gift! The title *Extravagant Graces* came to me—and never let go.

Last year, a new question popped into my mind: what would the children—now adults—say about their family featured in *Extravagant Graces*? So I asked them. You'll read their stunning answers in Part Two.

Jeanette Chaffee

Tualatin, Oregon
August 2014

JEANETTE CHAFFEE

While on TWA Flight 840, **JEANETTE CHAFFEE** survived the midair explosion of a terrorist bomb less than fourteen feet away from her. She has appeared on *CBS Evening News with Dan Rather, 20/20, The 700 Club*, and other television and radio shows. Jeanette has been quoted in *USA Today*, the *New York Times*, and *Newsweek*. She's authored diverse national magazine articles and is recognized as a gifted communicator. Jeanette hosted *Reflections*, a weekly radio show that aired in cities from South Carolina to the Arctic Circle.

You hold my life and
breath and eternal future
in Your loving hands.

Max Lucado

Terror in the Sky

Suspended midair between life and death

April 2, 1986: *What began as an ordinary travel day turned into sheer terror flying at seventeen thousand feet...*

BY JEANETTE CHAFFEE

I WAS JOLTED AWAKE BY AN EAR-SPLITTING, THUNDEROUS BOOM. It felt like a gun had been shot inches from my head. The plane lurched wildly. Swirling debris smothered me as smoke filled the cabin. Oxygen masks dropped. I yanked at mine—it wouldn't budge! Fear seized me. I told myself: *Don't panic. Look at how others have pulled their masks down. You can do this.*

Twenty-four hours earlier I'd been in Salem, Oregon, preparing for my trip to Greece and Turkey to purchase jewelry for my collectibles business. I wasn't even supposed to be on TWA 840. I'd changed my schedule when the travel agent found me an earlier flight—what could be wrong with starting my trip sooner?

At 4:30 a.m. on Tuesday, April 1, 1986, my brother-in-law dropped me off at the airport in Salem. Before I got out of the car, we prayed and I told him I'd be back in a few days.

Fifteen exhausting hours later, I arrived in Rome, Italy. Then I boarded the short leg to Athens. In the aisle seat of my row was an older Greek woman. She asked me in English, "Am I in 8C?"

Since I was in 8A by the window, I assured her she was in the correct place. The plane was filling up, but thankfully no one took the seat between us.

Lunch was chicken salad. We both ate, and then I stuffed a pillow against my window and drifted off to sleep.

We never spoke again.

The burnt smell reminded me of Fourth of July fireworks. My ears still rang from the tremendous explosion. The overhead bins had opened, and the lights were off.

I was now wide awake.

What happened? Where are we?

I saw an American man across the aisle with his oxygen mask on. Since mine wouldn't release, I jerked on the one above the empty seat next to me. It came down. Desperately, I stretched the elastic string over my head.

Comforted that at least I had the mask on, I turned to my window. I was stunned to see the tops of mountains *far* below. I had never felt so helpless.

I prayed: "Jesus, only You can help. Nobody even knows we're in trouble. Please, don't let us die."

Trying to get my bearings, I turned to my right. I saw blue sky through a nine-by-three-foot gaping hole in the side of the plane. To my horror, I realized the three rows of seats near the massive opening were now empty.

I hadn't heard a scream.

I was less than fourteen feet away.

The wind was rushing through the cabin, airplane insulation billowing. From the ceiling and the exposed panels around the rupture, dangled wires and tubes.

Mr. Taylor, a flight attendant, rushed down the aisle carrying a fire extinguisher. He passed me, but quickly realized that he shouldn't risk being sucked out. He retreated back to first class.

Another attendant came to my row. Desperately clutching the aisle seats, she stared at the empty space where seat 10F had been. She yelled, "Was anyone sitting there?"

"Don't you have a passenger list?" I shouted.

"Not onboard," she replied.

Flight attendant Cindy Purdy, only on the job for three weeks, came down the aisle and walked past the hole. I wondered why she dared.

A moment later, members of the crew were laying an elderly American woman across the seats in front of me. Her back was a mass of blood.

TWA Flight 840 after landing safely in Athens. Jeanette was sitting just two rows away from the terrorist bomb.

Her name was Myrtle. She was from Los Angeles. Her husband, Henry, was also badly injured.

She told me: "We were looking at each other when we saw a fireball. We knew we were going to die any second. We whispered 'I love you' to each other."

Since the seats next to me were empty, a young Saudi couple was moved to them. The wife was named Nahla. Her long dress was ripped off below the knee and her legs were horribly burned. She was wearing only one red shoe. Although her husband, Ibrahim, spoke some English and had traveled abroad before, she only spoke Arabic. This was her first time away from home.

Ibrahim was in a state of shock. He said he had seen passengers blasted out of the hole in the plane's side. I didn't want to believe it. *He's confused and hysterical*, I thought.

I tried to help Nahla, but what could I do? Would talking to her give her comfort?

***

Amid all the terror, there was no panic. No one screamed. There was no hysteria. Only a strange quiet existed amid the wild, roaring wind—as though we were suspended between life and death.

One of the crew members shouted: "We will be landing. We'll disembark using the steps, not the emergency chutes!"

It was a miracle we were still flying. I wasn't sure that we *could* land. And what if we ended up in the Mediterranean?

The engines whined as the plane lurched and shook. Would it hold together until we were on the ground? Did we have any landing gear left? As we started our descent, I silently prayed: *Come on, you can make it. Just stay in one piece a little longer. Jesus. Jesus. Jesus.*

We were fortunate because Captain Petersen was a pilot with thirty years experience. The landing was bumpy, but without incident. It was *almost* normal.

As the plane rolled down the runway, many passengers — including myself — started clapping and cheering.

"Thank You, Lord Jesus. Thank You, Lord Jesus," I gratefully prayed. I'd never been more sincere.

Out of my window, I saw fire engines and ambulances surrounding us.

People scrambled to exit, but the doors didn't open for an eternity. Eventually medics arrived to carry Myrtle and her husband, Nahla, and the other injured passengers off the plane. The rest of us weren't permitted to leave.

I stood on wobbly legs and moved to see who I could help. I discovered bits of wreckage were in my hair and on my blouse. No matter how much I brushed, I kept finding new pieces.

I noticed a man holding his head and crying for help. He told me his eyes were badly burned. I ran to the restroom. The tiny room had imploded and the walls were warped, but the sink still worked. Snatching a handful of paper towels, I doused them with water.

I rushed to the man. He kept saying, "My eyes hurt, my eyes," as he tried to soothe his pain with the wet towels. He said that flying pieces of shrapnel had kept hitting him. Oxygen masks at the back of the plane hadn't dropped and people had no protection from the blowing debris. Thank the Lord that He had provided for me.

Eventually, the 110 remaining uninjured passengers were allowed to disembark. People filed out serenely. I wanted to know what had happened, so I stayed on board.

I headed to the hole. Some of the flight crew and I studied the damage. I spotted a briefcase and Nahla's missing red shoe.

Mr. Taylor said, "It was a bomb."

I looked at him in disbelief. "That's not possible. Bombings don't happen to anyone I know."

Uniformed officials came aboard. "Get off," one man brusquely told me. They were worried there might be a second bomb.

The bomb ripped a huge hole in the side of the plane.

I handed my small Gideon New Testament to Cindy Purdy, the flight attendant. I said, "I'll pray for you."

Descending the metal stairs to the tarmac, I was shocked to see small puddles of blood. I thanked the Lord again that I was still alive.

We were all secured in an airport room. There were no telephones. Most of us were crammed together, sitting on the floor, or leaning against a wall.

How much longer will this chaos last? I wondered.

We received no updates.

Journalists were the only ones allowed to enter and speak with passengers. Just a handful of these interviews were broadcast back in the States where relatives would see that their loved ones were alive. I was fortunate enough to have my interview chosen.

Meanwhile, in Oregon, my family was frantic. Mom had heard a news alert regarding a plane explosion over Athens. Grabbing my itinerary, she was horror-struck to see it read "Flight 840."

All she knew was that people had been sucked out of the plane. I might have been one of them. A family member called church friends to pray. My relatives stayed glued to the television, anxiously awaiting any news.

During Dan Rather's evening broadcast, he explained that a terrorist bomb had exploded on Flight 840 from Rome to Athens, killing four and injuring seven. He cut to my interview.

"There she is. She's alive! She's alive!" Mom shouted. My appearance brought joy beyond words. The relief was bittersweet, knowing that people had perished, but she was grateful to God that I had survived.

_____

As my family learned my fate, I remained with all the other passengers in the room at the Athens airport for over ninety minutes. Uniformed officials stood on top of tables shouting instructions in Greek, which were translated into English.

"Stay put. No leaving yet. Write down your name and how many are in your party on these papers."

I hurried to add my name to the list.

Amid all this confusion, I talked to Ernie, the American who had been sitting across the aisle from me on the plane. He was a Christian and the Bible verses he quoted comforted me. He had been reading Psalm 91:11: "For He shall give His angels charge over you to keep you in all your ways."

At 6 p.m. I reached the hotel where others from the flight were staying. Television producers approached me, asking for an interview the next morning. This segment would appear on *20/20*. I agreed.

Although I was traumatized and fatigued, once in my hotel room I had to make a brief—and expensive—call home. I spoke to the first person who answered. My brother-in-law was grateful to hear from me. He reminded me of my prayer at the Salem airport: "Lord, please keep me safe from danger and protect me with Your angels."

After the call, I found a book with Scripture. One passage jumped off the page: "I trust in You, O Lord... My times are in Your hands (Psalm 31:14, 15)." I read and reread the verses.

God's Word brought me comfort as I thought of the four people who had died. A shepherd who had been interviewed on the TV news said he had "seen the sky raining bodies."

Three were members of one Greek-American family, including an eight-month-old baby, Demetra.

Alberto Ospina, from Connecticut, had changed his flight at the last minute—just like me. The bomb had been hidden under his seat, 10F, by someone unknown. His body was later found near Athens still strapped to his chair.

I was exhausted, but sleep was unthinkable. All through the night it was as if I was watching a video of the worst day of my life. When I closed my eyes, all I could see was an immense opening in the side of the plane. I was haunted by Myrtle's bloody back, Nahla's burned legs, and the man at the back of the plane pleading with me to help him with his hurting eyes.

It hit me. The Greek woman.

When I'd slept on the plane, she'd been within arm's reach. When I woke up, she was gone. *Where was she?*

At breakfast, I sought out Ernie because he'd sat so near the woman and me. "Where did that lady in 8C go? I never saw her after the explosion."

Ernie was eating cereal. He froze with the spoon halfway to his mouth. "I don't know. I never saw her again either."

I confirmed it with the airlines: they had no record of the Greek woman getting on or off the plane. That's when I believed. God had sent a guardian angel to protect the plane from disintegrating. After all, has a commercial plane ever landed safely following a midair bomb detonation?

After my experience on Flight 840, I was struck by the brevity of life. My relationship with Christ was *all* that mattered. I didn't think about what I looked like, what kind of car I drove, or the status of my bank account. I thought, *I'm glad I have the peace of God that "passes all understanding (Philippians 4:7)."*

Why did I survive when others near me didn't? All I know is that no guarantees of life exist, so I want to share with everyone that *now* is the time to personally accept Jesus as Savior.

WHO DID IT?

JUST a week before my fateful trip, the U.S. bombed the Libyan naval fleets in the Gulf of Sidra. In light of my plans, I prayed with Mom for my safety.

I was right to be concerned. The TWA bombing was in retaliation of that U.S. attack. The Arab Revolutionary Cells claimed responsibility. As relayed by the international press, a Lebanese woman was the primary suspect. She worked for the Abu Nedal Organization which had attempted to bomb a Pan American airplane in 1983.

Allegedly, she left the TWA bomb inside a life jacket under seat 10F during an earlier flight from Cairo to Athens. It is thought the bomb was a Czechoslovakian plastic explosive the size of a bar of soap.

If the bomb had gone off earlier or later, been closer to the wing, or had blown downward instead of outward — we all would have died.

Legal proceedings of passengers and families of victims were conducted as if the bomber's identity was confirmed. Yet nobody has ever been arrested, sued, or convicted for the bombing.

DON & CAROL RICHARDSON

From 1962 until 1977, **DON AND CAROL RICHARDSON** served as missionaries among a cannibal-headhunter tribe in Irian Jaya (now Papua, Indonesia). Their experiences have been recounted in the movie and book, *Peace Child.* (Those, and Don's other books, are available on Amazon.) *Peace Child* was featured as a *Reader's Digest* condensed book and was translated into more than thirty languages. Carol "graduated" to heaven in 2004. Don later met and married another Carol, who now serves in ministry with him. Don continues authoring books and traveling the world to teach about missions. He has four children and twelve grandchildren.

If you love until it hurts,
there can be no more
hurt, only more love.

Mother Teresa

Behind the Peace Child

Canoeing with a baby through crocodile-infested waters to live with cannibals

BY JEANETTE CHAFFEE

THE LORD PREPARED DON AND CAROL RICHARDSON FOR missions long before they lived in Irian Jaya (also called Dutch New Guinea). Don says, "Prior to falling in love with Carol, God had spoken to both of our hearts to know Him and to communicate the gospel to people who had never heard it before."

His future wife had this conviction since she was nine years old. Carol Soderstrom, a pastor's daughter from Cincinnati, attended a Bible camp in Louisiana. There she committed her life to missions.

Don became a Christian at age seventeen. Two weeks later, he heard a man speaking about sharing the gospel in remote areas. Don wanted to do what that man was describing.

He knew he would probably go to a "pretty wild" location.

"I told the Lord, 'There are probably not many women who would be willing to go to the kind of place I think I'm going. But if you can find one who loves You at least as much as I do and is willing to go anywhere You call us, and if You know she's right for me and I'm right for her, would You please triangulate to bring us together?'

"I added, 'And if she could be really pretty, that would be nice, too!'"

God answered that prayer when he met Carol at Prairie Bible Institute. Although Don was eager to marry her after their graduation in 1957, God called her to be a nurse and she wanted to finish her training first. Until she completed nursing school, Don pastored and conducted youth ministry. Then they married in 1960. After a year, they had their first child, Stephen.

Then the family moved to Irian Jaya. Don was interested in going to the distant swamplands to minister to the Sawi tribe of cannibal-headhunters, but worried that it was too much to ask of his wife. But God moved upon her heart and one day *she* made the suggestion that they move there. They rode for ten hours in a

Don in the boat he made—with his sons, Shannon, Paul, and Steve.

dugout canoe through crocodile-infested waters and became the first outsiders ever to reside with this violent tribe.

Don felt confident that they would not be harmed because no one from the outside world had hurt the Sawi. They wouldn't attack outsiders unless given reason.

"We encountered two hundred naked headhunter-cannibals brandishing spears and streaked with war paint. They welcomed us by dancing to the beat of their drums, chanting in a language of their own. This continued almost nonstop for three days and three nights.

Carol and baby Valerie in 1975.

"You can imagine what we felt like living in a twenty-by-twenty-foot thatched-roof house with our tiny baby and hardly any furniture." Until Don could make a bed, they slept on grass mats on the floor.

Since the natives didn't speak English and the Americans didn't speak Sawi, this caused some interesting and funny moments. The first five minutes of language study were baffling. Because in primitive tribes pointing with a finger is usually considered inappropriate, Don pointed with his chin to six items expecting to learn six different words. Instead, they gave him the same word all six times.

"I thought to myself, *Strange language!* I didn't realize they were giving me the word for *chin*."

While language learning progressed, Don and Carol soon discovered they were in a war zone. "We were horrified to see that the village up the river and the village where we lived were at war. The three-day welcome celebration was just an intermission."

Their hut was directly between the villages and they were caught in the crossfire. There were several close calls when the visitors were nearly impaled.

"I kept pleading with them to make peace. For six months, they would not honor that request. I finally said to the Sawi leaders, 'If you don't stop fighting, we will move to a different village.'"

This threat worried the villagers, as they liked Carol's medical help and Don's steel tools. In addition, the presence of white people gave them status.

Shortly after this, Don heard a woman wailing over her missing child. He asked her husband, "What have you done with your baby?"

Kaiyo responded: "I've given Biakadon as a peace child between our villages so your request will be honored. There won't be any bloodshed between our villages as long as my little son remains alive in the other village."

Don and a Sawi man in 1965.

The enemy village had also donated a baby in the other direction. As long as either son lived, there would be peace.

Don began thinking. *What's this? A father giving his son to reconcile with his enemies? There's something familiar about all of this….*

"I discovered an amazing parallel between God's redemptive plan for mankind and the Sawi culture. I recognized I could describe God's Son, Jesus, as the eternal peace child. He was given not as one father to another father. Rather, the heavenly Father gave His Son that all men may be at peace with Him and be reconciled to Him.

"As I described Jesus as the true peace child, the Bible verse we often quote at Christmas time came to mind — Isaiah 9:6, which says, 'Unto us a child is born, unto us a Son is given.'"

One of Christ's titles in this verse is Prince of Peace. To say this in Sawi, Don had to say *peace child*, because there is no other way to say it in that language.

"John 3:16 is the core of God's message. It says 'For God loved the world so much that He gave his only Son so that anyone who believes in Him shall not perish but have eternal life.' Thus, the Sawi understood the great meaning of God's peace child. The

The Richardsons: Steve, Shannon, Don, and Paul in June 2012, on their way to the Sawi 50th anniversary celebration in their honor.

very heart of the gospel was plain to them because of the parallel it had in their own culture."

One Sawi man told Don, "Your words make my liver quiver." This tribal expression means to have a desire aroused within one.

"He wanted to know how he could lay his hand on the peace child," Don says, "because the Sawi required each individual in the receiving village to lay his or her hand on the peace child and say, 'I receive this child as the basis of peace.'"

That man and many others began—by faith—"laying their hands" on Jesus Christ as their peace child.

Soon there were a few hundred Sawi Christians. Don translated the New Testament into their language. Then he trained other missionaries to continue teaching the Word to those believers.

After being away for several years, Don revisited the Sawi village. He found over 2,400 believers among 3,200 people in the tribe: a 75 percent conversion rate!

In June 2012, Don—accompanied by his sons Steve, Shannon, and Paul—returned to Irian Jaya for a joyful anniversary celebration of Don and Carol's first arrival fifty years earlier.

The Sawi tribe, estimated to be 85 percent Christian, hosted them. Four other tribes that the Sawi churches had been evangelizing also participated in the festivities. Three generations were represented. Many of those attending had been there when the Richardsons first arrived.

The celebration, with all the singing, dancing, worshiping, and baptizing, was unforgettable for Don.

"This was a culminating experience of my life thus far. God's Word has changed their lives."

DAVID STOOP

DAVID STOOP founded the Center for Family Therapy, where he is a Christian clinical psychologist. He obtained his master's degree at Fuller Seminary, where he's now an adjunct professor, and his PhD at the University of Southern California. He has published over thirty books, including *Forgiving Our Parents, Forgiving Ourselves*. He and Stephen Arterburn were the executive editors of *The Life Recovery Bible*, which has sold over 1.6 million copies. David received a Gold Medallion award from the Evangelical Christian Publisher's Association. He and Jan have been married for over fifty years. They have three grown sons and six grandchildren, and enjoy living in Newport Beach, California.

Everyone thinks of changing the world, but no one thinks of changing himself.

Leo Tolstoy

A Different Kind of Father

Living in denial, a man wants to be the father he never had

BY JEANETTE CHAFFEE

WHEN DAVID STOOP WAS TWENTY-TWO, HIS FATHER DIED. They had never been close. David never got the chance to really know his dad.

"There wasn't much for me to remember because he was a harsh disciplinarian and an absentee father. He was there *physically*, but he wasn't there *emotionally*. I thought this was normal; I didn't think much about it."

Living with absentee parents had left David emotionally cold, feeling lonely and abandoned. He had sometimes imagined he was adopted. *One day, my real parents will return for me, and everything will be fine.* Yet to everyone in the community, his family appeared to be normal.

With the birth of his own sons, David vowed, "I'm going to do it differently." Everything was fine when the boys were small. During the infant years—up until the "terrible twos" (which he now calls the "wonderful twos") — the boys were cuddly and fun. "They didn't have a will and didn't talk back."

Difficulties began when the kids entered elementary school and became uncooperative. Despite taking the time to coach Little League and going on frequent family outings, there was constant disappointment when he couldn't connect with his children.

"We ended up with the same distant relationship I had with my father." He kept thinking, *Maybe later we'll have the bond I long to have*.

Then Mike, his oldest son, graduated from high school. "The same longings kept resurfacing. I remember saying to myself, 'Wow... Mike's almost gone now. Maybe this will be the time I can connect with him.' But it just became harder instead of easier."

One day, David was jolted into reality when his son said: "Dad, you're *physically* here. But it's as if you have a sign saying 'Do Not Disturb.'"

David denied that. "No, no, no. You don't ask me questions or spend time with me. That's your fault, because I'm available."

Later, after his own healing, he confessed he could see Mike was right. "I wasn't there *emotionally* because I didn't know how to be there."

David's sister began talking to him about their dad's abusiveness. He didn't like what she was saying. He wouldn't admit that he'd never had a proper father. He argued with her because he didn't feel abused.

"I always said I had a great childhood because I had a lot of freedom." At the age of ten, he could go anywhere he wanted in the city if he had the bus fare. "My parents never even asked me where I'd been."

As much as he resented his sister's comments, David had to face reality. "I couldn't get out of my mind what she was saying. It started me thinking. I had refused to accept the unacceptable. I hadn't faced the truth."

At this moment, his healing began. It wasn't a quick fix. He took two years off of work to deal with the ramifications of denying his feelings for so long. When you do that in one part of your life, "you end up doing it with all parts of your life." Blocking bad feelings also meant blocking *good* feelings.

He had always told himself, "I'm not going to pay attention to feelings. I don't want any ups and downs." A graph of his emotions was simply a straight line.

He sought professional help. "Coming to terms with my feelings was like taking them out of the deep freeze. Bad stuff thaws first. You want to throw those feelings back in the freezer. If you have someone who can help you, then it's possible to keep them thawed out."

He acknowledged that the grieving process, which he did twenty years after his father's death, comes in stages. "After the denial, anger, and sadness comes acceptance."

David studied the Scriptures about forgiveness and the heart of God. He spoke about three of the myths of forgiveness.

One myth is that forgiveness should be quick and easy. However, it was thousands of years between Adam and Eve sinning in the garden of Eden, and the New Testament, when Jesus came to die on the cross to provide forgiveness.

Another myth is that forgiveness means there *must* be reconciliation. "An abusive situation is an example of when it should *not* take place." Forgiveness can happen without reconciliation, but reconciliation can *never* happen without forgiveness.

A third myth regarding forgiveness is that one should forget. But it's often helpful to remember events so that further injury will not occur.

During his two-year journey to make peace with his dad, he learned that "healing won't take place if one says the wound's not there."

The healing brought remarkable transformation to both himself and his family. "Something inside of me had changed. I was able to connect with them. I started to feel alive. My boys admit I'm a truly *present* father now. Even my wife says I'm a better husband!"

David wishes he could have talked frankly with his dad. He would have told him: "I really missed you. I wish I could have known you."

Now he does things with his own kids and grandkids that he didn't get to do with his dad. The Lord is reimbursing him, like it says in the book of Joel: "I will restore to you the years the locusts have eaten (2:25)."

One summer David and his son Mike met Mike's brothers in Europe. Greg was in Amsterdam working at Youth With a Mission and Eric was on vacation after a stressful bar exam. They rode city busses and trains, stayed in exotic places, and had a great time.

David told the boys he never would have been able to do these things ten years earlier.

"Why not?" Mike asked.

"Because after twenty minutes with you guys, I wouldn't have known what to do with you."

The mission statement David and his wife wrote after getting married — *to be agents of change and healing in relationships* — still resonates with him today.

The irony is that he himself needed to change. Forgiveness was the key to becoming a different kind of father.

STEPHEN ARTERBURN

STEPHEN ARTERBURN is the founder and chairman of New Life Ministries, the largest provider of professional Christ-centered counseling in the United States. Along with David Stoop, Steve hosts *New Life Live!* It's a radio talk show heard by two million people. He has written seventy books, including *The 7-Minute Marriage Solution*. Steve and David edited and produced *The Life Recovery Bible*. Steve founded the Women of Faith conferences attended by over four million. He serves on the board of the American Association of Christian Counselors.

He is a licensed minister and serves as a teaching pastor at Heartland Church in Indianapolis. ("I *love* to preach. I'd preach every Sunday if I could!") Steve and Misty have five children.

Getting over a painful experience is much like crossing monkey bars. You have to let go at some point in order to move forward.

C. S.Lewis

From Depression to Wholeness

A suicidal overeater becomes an inspirational speaker heard by millions

BY JEANETTE CHAFFEE

POOR SELF-ESTEEM PLAGUED STEVE ARTERBURN'S CHILDHOOD. "I often had feelings of inferiority," he admits. "I always had a sense of inadequacy. I needed to earn my acceptance, to earn my way. That's been the driving force of many things I have done. I wish it weren't so."

From a young age he didn't focus on the things that he *had*, but on what he *didn't* have. His life became a self-fulfilling prophecy. "I felt badly about myself and even worse when I gained weight." He still remembers the studio apartment where he sat watching television, gorging on high-fat foods, and living in isolation with the blinds pulled shut. "I was hopelessly depressed."

He has struggled with depression for much of his life. "In college, I was on antidepressants. I was suicidal a few times. I've had that to overcome."

Will I remain in despair all my life? He often wondered. *Is it possible for me to find a way out?*

Steve began transforming his life. At a seminar, he learned that making restitution would help him feel the grace God had given him. "I decided to do what everyone has to do who longs for significant changes in life: I surrendered."

He made a list of everyone he'd hurt and set about making things right. "My greatest obstacle has always been me. To have fulfillment in life, I have to get *me* out of the way." Steve gave up doing things his own way because he really wanted God's will.

"I can't do this. You can. I'm going to let You."

His faith brought amazing changes. "My journey led me to new nutritional patterns and eating habits." The result? He lost sixty pounds and has kept off the weight for over thirty-five years.

Steve isn't on antidepressants now, but he has to be careful. "If I don't take care of myself, get the right kind of rest, and watch what I eat, I can still get depressed. But it's not the kind of depression where I don't go to work or get dressed like it used to be." He's learned how to manage it.

As he discovered restoration in his own life, others responded to him. "I started counseling people in college. I've had a massive amount of problems in my own life to overcome. To my amazement, people felt comfortable approaching me for personal counseling." They sensed he understood their feelings and troubles.

In his seminars today, he addresses topics such as "Healing Is a Choice" and "Every Heart Restored." He still focuses on responding to the needs of those seeking restoration.

Steve's life can be summarized in six words: creativity, wisdom, generosity, compassion, perseverance, and integrity.

Integrity is being who you say you are. For Steve, it's important that people know he's a fellow struggler. If he didn't have integrity, folks could think that everything magically fit together in his life.

"Integrity means saying no to things you'd like to say yes to."
There are all sorts of reasons to *not* be a person of integrity. He
realizes he has to have people around him who hold him account-
able. "If I didn't have integrity, I don't think anyone would want
to work with me. I have to be the torchbearer of integrity or we'd
have a lot less wonderful people working in this organization."

The best surprise in his life came after seven years of trying to
start a family. He and his wife were told they would never be able
to have a child. They turned to adoption.

Steve and his daughter Madeline at her college graduation in 2013.

"One day, I was meeting with my publisher in Atlanta and out of the blue he asked me, 'What are you doing about children?' I shared with him our idea. 'My friend's daughter is pregnant and looking for a couple to adopt her baby,' he told me. We met with the young lady, and she decided she wanted us to have her child."

The girl was born in 1990. "Christmas Day we flew to Atlanta and got our daughter, Madeline. It was just wonderful!"

Despite all the hardships he faced, Steve never gave up. He accepted Christ's forgiveness and determined that all was not lost. He understood that God could use him in spite of his weaknesses.

"I had sinned. I had let Him down. Yet God still had a plan for me. I'm grateful—and surprised—for what Jesus has done by His grace."

Steve with two of his children, Solomon and Amelia.

EVELYN SAINT JIMENEZ & OLIVE FLEMING LIEFELD

EVELYN (SAINT) JIMENEZ was born and raised in Argentina, the child of missionary parents Phil and Ruth Saint. Her father was the brother of Nate Saint, one of the five missionaries murdered by Auca Indians in 1956.

Evelyn has authored five books on marriage and family life. She teaches couples, youth, and Bible students. Her husband, Humberto, pastors a church in Córdoba, where she is a family counselor. They have three grown children.

OLIVE (AINSLIE) FLEMING LIEFELD and Pete Fleming attended the same Plymouth Brethren Church in Seattle and were childhood sweethearts. They both attended the University of Washington.

Pete was encouraged to become a missionary by Jim Elliot, and the two went to Ecuador in 1951. Olive and Pete married in 1954, but sadly, their union lasted only eighteen months when he, Jim, and three others were killed.

Olive was recovering from her second miscarriage when she learned of her husband's death. After a visit to the U.S., she returned to Ecuador to assist one of the five widows, Marilou McCully, in caring for her three young boys. Olive authored *Unfolding Destinies: The Ongoing Story of the Auca Mission.*

After she returned to the United States, she met and married Dr. Walter Liefeld, a professor at Trinity Evangelical Divinity School. They live in Illinois and have three adult children.

*He is no fool who gives
what he cannot keep, to
gain what he cannot lose.*

Jim Elliot, 1949

Evelyn and her husband, Humberto.

Speared: Betrayed by New Friends

They came in peace...

BY JEANETTE CHAFFEE

WHY WOULD GOD PLANT THE DESIRE FOR MISSIONS INTO the hearts of five remarkable Americans — have them travel thousands of miles into one of the most remote jungles in the world — only to let them be senselessly slaughtered? Fifty years later, the answer is revealed.

THE FAMILIES

IN 1956, five men attempted contact with the Auca (now known as the Waorani), a remote Ecuadorian tribe known to be among the most vicious in the world. The men's single purpose was to tell the tribe about the love of Christ.

On January 8, the Auca attacked without warning. Nate Saint, Pete Fleming, Ed McCully, Roger Youderian, and Jim Elliot were brutally killed.

NATE SAINT was a builder, inventor, and skilled pilot. His dream of being a fighter pilot was dashed when the Army rejected him from their flight program, saying that an injury when he was a teenager made him ineligible. However, he remained in the Army and served in World War II.

After the war, he went to Wheaton College. There he met Marj, a nursing student. They fell in love and married. Interested in ministry, the couple investigated Mission Aviation Fellowship (MAF). To Nate's great joy, he was qualified to fly the organization's small planes. Evelyn remembers her dad saying that "it was such a relief when Uncle Nate discovered he could be a pilot after all."

Nate and Marj joined MAF and arrived in Ecuador in 1948. They lived in Shell Mera where there was an airstrip which he could use as a base. Marj stayed at home to operate the radio. She kept in touch with Nate while he was flying food and medical supplies, and transporting missionaries. She was also the center of all communication in the area since phones didn't exist in the jungle.

Soon they were blessed with three children, Kathy, Steve, and Philip. Nate's sister, Rachel, came to visit. She loved Ecuador and decided to join him as a missionary. Being a linguist, she thought it would be great to translate the Bible into local languages.

Nate's older brother, Phil, also wanted to be a missionary. He'd attended Wheaton College where he met and married Ruth. He and Ruth were attending language school in Costa Rica when Nate was murdered.

Phil was a preacher, itinerant evangelist, and gifted artist—despite being partially color blind. He sketched pictures and chalk drawings on portable blackboards.

Such talent ran in the family. Lawrence Saint, their father, was a master of stained glass. He received a commission for two windows for the Washington National Cathedral in D.C. One depicted the Bible story of the boy with the loaves and fish. Nate was five at the time and his father used him as the model.

Phil and Ruth had six children. The youngest, Evelyn, was born in Argentina three years after her Uncle Nate's death. She talks about how it deeply impacted her family growing up.

"Dad felt he 'was carrying the torch for Uncle Nate.' Dad was always either preaching or sharing the story, so it was embedded

Phil Saint drawing for watching Auca, with his sister Rachel standing behind him.

in my heart. He always drew the beach landing on his chalkboard. I thought it was an amazing — though sad — story. The men were so young! They left entire families behind."

To this day Evelyn can still vividly picture her dad's nine-foot Auca spear on their living room wall.

———————

PETE FLEMING became a Christian at age thirteen through the testimony of a blind evangelist. Olive Ainslie grew up in Seattle. They attended the same church and were childhood sweethearts. Both attended the University of Washington where Pete earned a master's degree in American Literature.

He met Jim Elliot through a Christian student organization. They enjoyed mountain climbing in the Pacific Northwest and spent time talking about their futures. Jim told Pete about his dream to contact the Auca and encouraged him to go to Ecuador.

The two bachelors traveled by ship to Quito in 1951. They both had to leave behind the women they loved. Eventually Pete

San Pedro, Calif. '51

Pete Fleming and Jim Elliot ready to ship off for Ecuador.

proposed to Olive by letter and they were married in the States in 1954. She followed him back to Ecuador, never dreaming she would be a widow within eighteen months.

ED MCCULLY grew up in Milwaukee. His dad was a bakery executive. Ed enrolled in Wheaton College and majored in business and economics. He was a star football player and ran on the track team. An outstanding speaker, he won a national oratorical contest, and was chosen to be the senior class president. While at Wheaton, he met Jim Elliot and they became great friends.

After graduating, Ed was admitted to Marquette University Law School. He still kept in touch with Jim, who was making plans to leave for Ecuador. During this time, Ed was working as a hotel night clerk. This job gave him plenty of quiet moments in which he could read the Bible — particularly the book of Nehemiah — and think about Jim's commitment to the Auca.

Ed no longer wanted to be a lawyer, so the day before registration for his second year, he dropped out. He contacted Jim, and the two began traveling and speaking at churches around the country. They also hosted a weekly Christian radio program.

On a visit to Michigan, he met Marilou Hoboth, who was a graduate of Moody Bible Institute. They married in 1951.

In preparation for the mission field, Ed was studying dentistry, obstetrics, and tropical diseases at Biola College. The next year they left for the jungles of Ecuador with their eight-month-old son.

ROGER YOUDERIAN was raised on a Montana ranch. He joined the army, where he was a paratrooper and fought at the Battle of the Bulge. He was also in General Eisenhower's honor guard.

After his military service, he attended Northwestern School in Minneapolis, where he met Barbara Orton. They married and he studied missionary medicine. Along with their two small children, they moved to southern Ecuador and lived with the savage Jivaro Indians, who were famous for shrinking heads.

JIM ELLIOT was from Portland, Oregon. He was popular at his high school, where he was an influential leader. He attended Wheaton College. He was a top wrestler and an excellent student. While there, he met another Greek major, Elisabeth Howard. The two enjoyed walks and had long talks while drinking Coke. They fell in love.

Jim in 1951.

However, God wanted Jim to remain single. Jim was up front with Elisabeth and told her he had no idea if he'd ever get married. Because of this, they separately went to Ecuador as single missionaries. They still saw each other

Elisabeth and Jim.

when they could, and enjoyed sightseeing and studying Spanish together.

When their mission work kept them apart, they wrote long letters to each other. Eventually God gave Jim the green light and the couple married on October 8, 1953.

OPERATION AUCA

OLIVE Fleming remembers vivid stories about the bloodthirstiness of the Auca. Despite the dangers, she and Pete wanted to reach them. Along with several other missionaries, a secret plan was formed to bring God's love to these violent people.

ABOUT THE AUCA

The Auca Indians lived isolated from all other cultures. For centuries they had been murdering everyone who entered their territory. They thought *all* outsiders were cannibals—even peaceful foreigners.

Murder was commonplace among their own people. Any reason to kill was a good one: an argument, having bad luck, anticipating an attack by other Auca groups, an illness or injury or physical defect, trading with a *cowode* (outsider), hoarding food, or stealing a wife. Their favorite pastime was telling stories about wielding their machetes and bamboo spears.

Each man had distinctively decorated spears. That was how the warriors knew who killed who—important for awarding status. The Auca held vendettas and *never* forgot a grudge.

Prior to an attack, everything in the village was made to appear normal. The warriors didn't dance or put on face paint. This wasn't warfare—it was deception. The Auca prided themselves on sneak attacks and never letting the enemy have any chance to fight back. They wanted all the odds in their favor.

SHELL MERA

In the 1930s, oil, rubber, and logging companies were highly interested in finding natural resources in the Amazon rainforest. Many were willing to go to almost any length for access and therefore often ran into conflict with the area natives. In 1937, the Shell Oil Company built a town just outside Auca territory and constructed an airstrip. During the next eleven years, the company tried to explore the region, but several of its employees were killed by Indians. Eventually Shell abandoned what had become known as Shell Mera.

This was the year Nate and Marj Saint arrived in Ecuador. They were delighted to find homes already built, courtesy of Shell! Other missionaries soon joined them and the community thrived.

SECRET PLANS

Olive recalls how important the foundation of prayer was in reaching the Auca. She'd often heard her husband Pete say, "I am longing now to reach the Auca if God gives me the honor of proclaiming His Name among them." For years before moving to Ecuador, Jim Elliot had been praying, "God, send me to the Auca."

Jim also prayed: "Over the Auca, Father, I want to sing!"

Ed McCully joined the men in their dedication. Together they recruited Nate Saint, as he'd been in Ecuador the longest and had the most influence.

They called their project Operation Auca. Its mission was to make contact with these remote people and bring them the gospel. Olive remained apprehensive because she knew Operation Auca must be kept secret. The concern was

An Auca longhouse in the jungle.

that if word leaked, outside companies would ruin the mission by getting involved. Not even the wives knew all their husbands' plans until later.

The fifth and final member to join was Roger Youderian. The others knew he'd had experience with violent tribes. He was also a map creator, a skill which would help Nate, the pilot, navigate the jungles.

Plans were progressing, but two huge problems remained unanswered. There wasn't a place for the plane to set down. The single-engine Piper had no pontoons for water landing and the jungle was impenetrable without an airstrip.

The other problem was that no one knew exactly where the Auca lived. The tribe was nomadic. Though Nate frequently flew over villages, they often were unoccupied. There were also other people in the jungle who weren't Auca. Finding the reclusive natives wouldn't be easy.

Both questions were answered late that summer. One day Ed and Nate were flying with some Quichua Indian passengers. Suddenly one of them started yelling, "Auca! Auca!" The Quichua had spotted their traditional enemy down below.

While the Indians were terrified with the find, the missionaries were ecstatic. The men silently prayed: *Lord, thanks for this moment. Please guide us to contact them before they disappear.*

It was time to act. Should they travel by canoe? It could take weeks. But would it be possible to build a landing strip in the dense jungle? Either option would take time, and by then the Auca might have moved on.

The men did the only thing they knew: Jim led them in prayer that the God of the Impossible would make a way. Then they sang their favorite hymn, "We Rest on Thee. "

MAKING NEW FRIENDS

Nate had an idea. He wanted to lower a bucket on a rope from his plane. Normally this wouldn't work without a helicopter, because the bucket would move with the plane. However, he calculated that if he flew in a tight enough circle, with the bucket-rope in the center, he could keep it stationary long enough for an Auca to untie a gift. This would be a great way to make friends with them until they could figure out a way to reach them in person.

Fortunately, Nate was a terrific pilot. Performing his bucket drop maneuver would be dangerous and difficult, but he figured it out. Adding a bag of rock salt to the bucket made it heavier and steadier.

Despite his seven years experience in the jungle, he was always careful. Olive remembers him saying, "Every time I take off, I am ready to deliver up the life I owe to God."

That fall it was time for the real test. Nate flew to the Auca's last known location. The Americans shouted one of the few phrases of Auca they knew: "Biti miti punimupa." *I like you; I want to be your friend.*

Once they'd attracted the attention of some Auca, they lowered the bucket with gifts of colorful shirts, axe-heads, kettles,

An Auca encampment near the river.

and trinkets. The Auca were delighted with their prizes and the missionaries felt Nate's idea had been a success.

The weekly bucket drops continued for three months. One day the bucket seemed extra heavy as they pulled up the rope. It was a gift—a parrot from the Auca! It became a much-loved pet to Stevie Saint and Valerie Elliot.

During these weekly flyovers, Nate noticed a sandbar on the river. It occurred to him that he might be able to land on it.

Olive explains: "It was a miracle. Normally it rained for months, raising the river level to cover all sand surfaces."

The men nicknamed the tiny strip of land "Palm Beach."

Everyone felt urgent pressure that *this* was the time to meet the Auca. The jungles were unpredictable and rain could return at any moment, washing away the sandbar landing strip.

THE KILLINGS

SEVERAL missionary families gathered at the Elliot's home between Christmas and New Year's 1955 to finalize plans for the first landing at "Palm Beach."

The McCully's home in Arajuno would serve as home base since it was nearest the jungle. Barbara Youderian and her kids kept Ed's wife, Marilou, company. The children played together, unaware of the impending danger.

Elisabeth and ten-month-old Valerie lived near the Saints in Shell Mera. Since Marj Saint would be manning the radio, her home would be the communication center. Olive was sick, so she stayed with Marj.

Unfortunately, the Saints had guests visiting that week, so the wives had to be extra careful not to leak the secret Operation Auca plans. At least the radio was in a different room, but since radio waves were public, anything private had to be in code. Olive knew that "Terminal City" was the Auca village Nate had spotted from the air. The message — "expected to have an early afternoon service" — meant "we saw Auca on the path."

On January 3, 1956, Olive said good-bye to Pete as he left for Arajuno to join the others. She was glad to hear he landed safely.

The next day Nate made five 30-minute round trips between Arajuno and "Palm Beach," transporting the men and the supplies they needed. These included food, a harmonica, flashlights, a yo-yo, and two-way radios. They also brought along a View-Master with picture reels to show their visitors.

A pre-fabricated tree house was installed thirty-five feet above ground. Roger, Jim, and Ed slept in it. When they climbed down from the tree the next morning, they spotted puma footprints. They were glad for their safe retreat.

On the men's first full day in Auca territory, the missionaries gathered along the Curaray River to sing their special song.

We rest on Thee, our Shield and our Defender,
Thine is the battle, Thine shall be the praise;
When passing through the gates of pearly splendor,
Victors, we rest with Thee through endless days.

Every night Pete flew back to Arajuno with Nate. He was chosen because he weighed the least. They had decided to do this in case the river flooded or the camp was attacked. This also allowed them to bring back the film of the photos they'd taken that day. Once they delivered a love note from Jim to his Elisabeth. She didn't know it would be her last communication with him.

Each morning, Pete and Nate returned to "Palm Beach" carrying the meals that Barbara and Marilou had prepared.

Friday was quiet. Jim fished in the river and proudly held up his catch for a photo shoot. His friends floated in the river. The water brought relief from the sweltering heat.

That afternoon, Jim looked over at the forest. To his delight, three Auca emerged. *I've dreamed about this day for years*, he thought.

According to Nate Saint's diary, Jim smiled and walked part way across the river to meet the guests. He said "I like you" in Auca, and they returned the greeting. Jim guided them to meet his partners. The missionaries excitedly repeated the few Auca phrases they had memorized.

The two women were named Gimade and Mintake. The man was Nenkiwi. He was wearing his brightly colored shirt—a gift from a bucket drop.

Nate showed them the airplane. Astonishingly, they weren't afraid of it. Nenkiwi was fascinated with the "wood-bee," as he called the Piper. That was all Nate needed.

He persuaded the man to go for a flight—which turned into two. Nenkiwi shouted with delight during the ride. For the first time he viewed his village by air. Spotting one of his fellow warriors, he said in Auca, "Mincaye, why are you so small down there? The 'wood-bee' flies so fast and everyone looks like ants!"

They circled and descended. But Nenkiwi wouldn't let Nate stop. Off they went again.

When they eventually landed, Nate remembered the two wooden model planes he had built. He'd given one to his son, but he had a spare. He presented the three-foot toy to his new friend as a goodwill gift. Everyone appeared to be having a good time. All seemed peaceful.

SPEARED

No visitors came on Saturday. Returning home after a quiet day, Pete sensed a change. Nate's diary reported, "Flying over the village, I knew something was different today."

Before leaving for "Palm Beach" Sunday morning, Pete made a rare radio call to Olive. "Pray. I'm sure this is the day."

"And it was the day," Olive says. "Pete and I had recently read 2 Corinthians 5:5 together. It says, 'He who has prepared you for this very thing is God.' This greatly encouraged me."

Nate radioed Marj. "We're expecting visitors this afternoon. I'll call you at 4:35 p.m."

Meanwhile, the Auca village was full of drama. Nenkiwi wanted to take Gimade as his third wife against the will of the tribal leaders. After the couple left the missionaries on Friday, they crept away into the jungles alone. Word of this wrongdoing got back to the tribe and he was sentenced to die.

In order to save his life, he lied, claiming that he and Gimade had only gone into the forest to escape the foreigners who had attacked them.

Gikita, the tribal leader, stirred his men to violence by shouting: "We have to kill the white men. They must die. Come on. Have courage and don't be afraid. This is not the time to be a coward."

Five warriors stepped up to his call. Their names were Kimo, Diewe, Namp, Nimonga, and Mincaye.

The men spent Sunday afternoon by the river. Four tribal women showed up, talking and approaching the men. *How strange that no men came with them. Anyway, it's another chance for us to make friends*, Pete thought.

The women investigated the plane to distract the missionaries, while six Auca warriors suddenly attacked the men from behind.

The white men had guns for protection from the wildlife, but they refused to use them against the Auca.

Within minutes, Ed McCully, Nate Saint, and Jim Elliot lay dead, bamboo spears protruding from their backs. Roger

Youderian made it to the plane and was about to radio for help when he was speared.

Olive explains, "My husband was the last one to die."

Pete headed for the river to get away. Standing on a log, he turned and saw Kimo chasing him with a nine-foot hardwood spear.

"Why are you doing this?" Pete asked in Auca. "I want to be your friend."

Gikita, the Auca chief who made the decision to kill the American missionaries, including pilot Nate Saint, also pictured. Drawing by Phil Saint.

Kimo then speared him.

Elisabeth Elliot describes the horrific murders: "The men were all on the beach. Auca suddenly leaped out of the forest and killed them immediately. I suppose our husbands jumped back into the water hoping to evade the sudden shower of spears."

For six years her husband had prayed for the Auca, and those very people had murdered him and his friends.

For Elisabeth and the other wives, losing their husbands "meant everything in life and continues to mean that. To these people, killing five men was little more than routine."

At 4:35 p.m., the missionary women were waiting by their radios.

Silence.

By 4:45 p.m., Olive and Marj knew something was wrong. Nate *never* missed a check-in. Marj radioed for help.

However, it was too late in the day for airplane travel. An air rescue would have to wait until sunrise.

The next morning one of the MAF pilots picked up Barbara Youderian and they flew over "Palm Beach." She spotted the Piper on the sandbar—the wings had been stripped. There was no sign of the men.

HCJB, the Christian radio station in Quito, broadcast the news that the five men were missing.

On Tuesday, the U.S. Air Force dispatched a rescue party on foot. Several missionaries joined the trek. A couple of days later four bodies were discovered downstream from "Palm Beach." (Quichua Indians later found Ed McCully's body.) There were a few personal belongings of the men including a camera, wedding rings, and Nate's watch—which had stopped at 3:10 p.m.

While soldiers stood guard, a hole was dug and the bodies were placed inside. A short prayer was given. The funeral was brief because night was approaching and the search team was worried the Auca would return.

The wives were gathered at Marj's home waiting for news. "We were sitting around the kitchen table, some holding our little ones," Olive remembers. "Then we were widows."

After learning that the men were dead, the women read in the Bible about heaven. They sang the hymn their husbands loved to sing, "We Rest on Thee."

We rest on Thee, our Shield and our Defender,
Thine is the battle, Thine shall be the praise;
When passing through the gates of pearly splendor,
Victors, we rest with Thee through endless days.

Evelyn Saint's Uncle Nate died at the age of thirty-three. "My parents were learning Spanish in Costa Rica at the time. Uncle Nate's death had a profound impact on my dad. Deeply moved, he solemnly renewed his dedication to his calling."

Jim and Elisabeth, newlyweds in Ecuador.

TRANSFORMATIONS

THE press worldwide covered the deaths of the Americans. *Reader's Digest* and *Life* publicized the story in America. For months, Olive received mail from people asking about Pete and the other men.

There was even more publicity a year later when Elisabeth Elliot published *Through Gates of Splendor*, a book about the martyrs, which became a best-seller.

A few months before Jim was killed, Elisabeth told him she was gathering photos, letters, and all sorts of information about him. "One day I will write your biography."

He laughed and went back to reading his magazine. *Shadow of the Almighty: The Life and Testament of Jim Elliot* came out in 1958.

THE WOMAN WHO STARTED IT ALL

Evelyn's Aunt Rachel was in Ecuador when her brother Nate died. She was working with a remarkable young Auca woman named Dayuma. She'd escaped from her tribe ten years earlier when her father was murdered. Dayuma became the first Auca to know the Lord. It was through her that Rachel Saint was able to learn the Auca language and teach her brother the native phrases the men used in Operation Auca.

About two years after the missionaries were speared, two women from Dayuma's tribe found her. She'd had no contact with her village since running away. The women explained that her mother was desperate to see her.

Dayuma traveled with them to her village. People were amazed, as they assumed she'd been eaten by the white foreigners. She told them that the murdered missionaries had come with a message of peace: they had weapons, but didn't use them, just as God had the power to stop Jesus from being crucified, but didn't. Dayuma explained, "Just as you killed the foreigners on the beach, Jesus was killed for you."

This was revolutionary. Self-sacrifice was not a part of the Auca culture. They were all about revenge—holding grudges and killing—and couldn't imagine another lifestyle. *Strange white people*, they thought.

Dayuma returned to Evelyn's Aunt Rachel a few weeks later. She didn't come alone. Five Auca women and their children accompanied her, singing "Jesus Loves Me."

The Indian women brought an unexpected invitation from the Auca leaders. "We did wrong to kill those five *cowodi* [outsiders]. We want to learn to live well. We want to learn to know

Dayuma, the first Auca Christian, and missionary Rachel Saint. Drawing by Phil Saint.

Waengongui [Creator God]. Tell them we'll build a house for them. Tell them to come!"

Rachel discussed this extraordinary opportunity with Elisabeth. Would they be crazy to go live with the people who had killed their relatives?

For many days the group canoed up rivers and trekked through the thick jungles. Elisabeth had brought along three-year-old Valerie. Each night they hung hammocks, but sleep didn't come easily as they heard chittering monkeys and growling pumas. They were also concerned about what would happen when they arrived at their destination.

Should they have accepted the invitation from a tribe that honored deception? Could the Auca be trusted?

They could only pray for God's protection as they drew closer to Dayuma's village.

Suddenly a band of Auca warriors appeared, blocking their way. Each man carried a decorated spear. The women froze. Valerie gripped her mommy's hand. Even she sensed the danger.

A fearsome warrior stepped forward. His name was Kimo. The women didn't know he was the man who had speared Pete Fleming to death.

Without a word, he laid his spear on the ground.

Healing had begun.

MIRACULOUS BAPTISMS

Elisabeth and Valerie lived with the Auca until 1961. Early on, Elisabeth wrote to the other widows. "In the initial stages of introducing what it means to be a follower of Christ... I can trust and believe that the prayers of thousands are yet to be answered in the way God wants them to be."

Over time God answered those prayers in ways few would have believed possible. Not only did many Auca become Christians—but *even the six killers gave their hearts to the Lord!*

As leaders, these men were highly influential, and when they promised that their generation would not kill again, they kept their word.

Two of Nate Saint's young children, Kathy and Steve, spent summers visiting their Aunt Rachel in the Auca village. It was like a three-month camping trip. The kids had fun living in her thatched hut and helping with the cooking. Kathy saw first-hand the change in the lives of the killers.

"I got to know Kimo and Diewe, two of the killers, because their huts were nearby. These two men were church leaders who profoundly influenced my life. I grew to love them."

Kathy requested to be baptized and the leaders agreed. The baptism was all set to take place in a village named Tiwaeno, but weather intervened.

"This was all God's doing. My brother and I made a first-time-ever trip to 'Palm Beach' to see where our dad had been killed. While there, rainstorms back at the village caused the

Phil Saint with Aucas.

men to suggest that we go ahead and have the baptismal service right away. Kimo and Diewe baptized me, along with Steve and two Auca children, near the grave of my dad and the other four missionaries. I did not choose to have Dad's killers baptize me, but I loved these men and was thrilled that they were chosen."

Other killers were similarly changed.

Evelyn said her father, Phil, twice baptized Auca Christian converts—including Mincaye, his brother's murderer.

Mincaye admitted: "We acted badly, badly until they brought us 'God's Carvings' [the Bible]. Now we walk *Waengongui's* [Creator God's] trail."

Gikita, the leader of the killers, told Rachel, "Then my heart was full of hate, but now it is healed!"

Phil was moved and amazed. "I baptized Mincaye in the river. He's my brother in Christ! How can I doubt God's power when I see Auca killers praying?"

Evelyn Saint never got to meet her uncle, but loved him through the stories she heard. She often thought about him giving his life for Jesus. The Auca spear that hung on her parents' living room wall was not a grim reminder of death, but a symbol of triumphant obedience.

God took his five loyal servants home, but through their sacrifice, generations of lives have been transformed.

FROM THE MARTYRS' MEMORIAL SERVICE
QUITO, ECUADOR • JANUARY 15, 1956

"I have fought a good fight, I have finished my course, I have kept the faith." **2 TIMOTHY 4:6-8**

Cloud of Witnesses

Discovering secrets thirty years after her husband's murder

BY JEANETTE CHAFFEE

COMPOSER RON OWEN SAT AT HIS PIANO. HE WAS WORKING on the score for the upcoming film, *End of the Spear*, which was scheduled for release in 2005. A few years earlier he'd done the soundtrack for *Beyond the Gates of Splendor*. That was a documentary about the five missionaries who were killed in the Ecuadorian jungle in 1956—the new dramatic film was about the same people, but he wanted its music to be different.

Struggling with ideas, he prayed that God would bless the project. Fingering the keys, he began experimenting with melodies. Soon he was developing a song that would become "You Led Me." He had no idea of the miraculous nature of the tune he was composing.

Olive Fleming Liefeld returned in 1989 to Ecuador, where her husband had died thirty-three years earlier. Pete Fleming, along with four other missionaries, had been killed by Auca Indians. Olive was to visit the site of the murders—"Palm Beach," a small sandbar used as a landing field—for the first time. She was accompanied by her son and second husband, and hoped to learn more details about Pete's death.

In the years since Olive had left, many of the Auca—including all of the murderers—had become Christians. She was able to talk to them and learn information that had been secret for decades. Her first question was the one that had never been answered: *why* had the men been killed?

She learned that an Auca named Nenkiwi had visited the Americans at "Palm Beach." The missionaries had made camp there in the hopes of communicating with the reclusive tribe. Pilot Nate Saint had given Nenkiwi plane rides in the "wood-bee." The native acted friendly and everything seemed fine when he left.

However, he was interested in one of the two women who had accompanied him. The tribe disapproved of him marrying Gimade, and when the leaders found the couple alone together, they prepared to execute him as punishment.

To escape this fate, Nenkiwi lied, putting the blame on the missionaries. "They were attacking us! We had to get away from the *cowodi* [outsiders] because they were going to kill us."

Gikita, the tribal leader, decided that the five foreigners had to die, and six warriors speared the white men to death in an unprovoked attack. This was the first time Olive knew the truth of why her husband had died. Nenkiwi's selfish lie had cost the peaceful Americans their lives.

Nenkiwi's reprieve was only temporary—a few years later the tribe buried him alive. Auca tradition meant his youngest was supposed to die with him, but Tementa escaped.

"Tementa is now a strong Christian," Olive says. "While we were there, he read us a passage from Mark and told us a Bible story." She was continually amazed at all God had accomplished.

A few days after that, she met the man who had actually killed Pete. Kimo was now a Christian. His wife's name was Dawa, and she'd been one of the decoys who distracted the white men so they could be ambushed.

"Dawa was the second Auca to become a Christian."

Olive had been warned not to ask specific questions about the murders. Instead she simply brought up the topic of "Palm Beach" — the sandbar used as an airstrip where the martyrs had died — and hoped the native couple would reveal something. To her surprise, they gave her astonishing new information.

"While we were spearing the five men we heard music coming from heaven," Kimo explained. "We were terrified."

Dawa was also a witness. "After the killing I saw many white people singing above the trees. The sky was full of jungle beetles with very bright lights that didn't blink. I heard strange music and singing. I was afraid."

Their fear of the angelic vision made sense to Olive. In the superstitious Auca culture, spiritual matters always meant bad things: the spirits meted out punishment. There was no positive aspect of spirituality, such as love.

She also understood that hearing music was extraordinary. The Auca had no music. It was only now, after missionaries brought them songs, they could even describe what they had heard so many years before.

Other Auca verified Kimo and Dawa's account. The killers lived far apart and had no way of communicating with each other, so the community believed their reports were accurate.

Olive's discovery was only the beginning of extraordinary revelations to come. A dozen years after her visit, work was in progress to make a movie about the murders.

"A producer and Steve Saint [whose father was one of the martyred] were in the jungle in Ecuador to film *End of the Spear,*" Olive explains. "They were listening to music that was going to be in the movie."

All of a sudden, Kimo — the killer of Pete — became frantic. "That's what we heard! That's what we heard!"

Steve asked, "What do you mean?"

"That's what we heard when we were killing the men."

The strange music in the sky that the Auca warriors heard in 1956 and couldn't describe was now revealed as the song that composer Ron Owen had just written for the modern-day film. Somehow God allowed the Auca to hear "You Led Me" *before* Ron Owen created it half a century later.

Their souls went to heaven And to angels' delight
They joined in the chorus Of heavenly light.

From poem by Joyce Hulstedt (in-law to Jim Saint)

The author with the watercolor of *Cloud of Witnesses,* later redone as an oil painting (shown on the next page).

> We are surrounded by so great a cloud of witnesses... looking unto Jesus, the author and finisher of our faith... HEBREWS 12:1–2

THE OIL PAINTING

PHIL Saint (brother of martyr Nate Saint) heard about the angels the Auca had seen above the trees during the spearing. He painted a picture representing singers in the sky. He titled it *Cloud of Witnesses*.

His daughter Evelyn will never forget February 12, 1993. "Dad called. He excitedly told me he'd just finished painting it." That evening her father was tragically killed in a freak tractor accident.

"Dad left the legacy of the painting. I signed his name on it—the only detail missing."

Evelyn and her mother, Ruth, later presented it to Dr. Pat Robertson and *The 700 Club*.

THE KILLERS' VOICES

KIMO, receiving first Bible:

"Father God, You are alive... We want all of Your Carvings [the Bible]."

GIKITA, after accepting Jesus:

"I used to hate and kill, but now the Lord has healed my heart."

GIKITA, shortly before his death in 1997, talking about how he will see in heaven the men he killed:

"I will just wrap my arms around them and laughing and happy we will live together in peace."

MINCAYE, killer of Nate Saint:

"My heart was dark like night, but Jesus... came and washed it."

"Now we walk His trail."

THE MARTYRS' VOICES

ROGER YOUDERIAN:

"I want to be a witness for Him, following
Him every second of my life."

PETE FLEMING:

"I am longing now to reach the Auca if God gives me
the honor of proclaiming His name among them."

ED MCCULLY:

"I pray that God will spare the lives of these Indians."

NATE SAINT:

"When the Lord Jesus asks us to pay the
price... we often answer 'it costs too much.'
Yet God didn't hold back His only Son."

"I am ready to deliver up the life I owe to God."

JIM ELLIOT, at Wheaton College, 1948:

"God, send me to the Auca."

"Father, take my life... have it all."

"Live to the hilt every situation you
believe to be the will of God."

ELISABETH ELLIOT &
VALERIE ELLIOT SHEPARD

ELISABETH ELLIOT and her husband, Jim, were serving as missionaries in Eastern Ecuador when he was brutally murdered by the Auca Indians (now known as Waorani) in 1956. She was left alone with a baby daughter, Valerie. Later, she spent two years living with the tribe who killed her husband. She is a world-renowned speaker, has authored over twenty books, and hosted a national radio show.

VALERIE (ELLIOT) SHEPARD was born in Shell Mera, Ecuador. She and her mother lived with the Quichua Indians, who named her *Pilipinto* (which means "butterfly"). In 1963 they moved to New Hampshire. For thirty-eight years Valerie has been married to Walter Shepard, a pastor. She homeschooled their eight children, and speaks at retreats and teaches Bible classes. They live in North Carolina.

*Few delights can equal
the mere presence of one
whom we trust utterly.*

George MacDonald

You've Gone Too Far This Time, God

Isolated in the Amazon jungle with a three-year-old daughter

BY JEANETTE CHAFFEE

THE TREK INTO THE ECUADORIAN JUNGLE TOOK SEVERAL arduous days via winding trails and dugout canoes. Elisabeth Elliot and her three-year-old daughter, Valerie, were returning to their primitive home deep in the rain forest. Every night on their journey they slept in a hammock strung up in palm leaf huts.

One morning they were traveling up a flooding river and it was bitterly cold. Elisabeth knew they would be miserable.

"It's hard for people to think of South American tropical jungles as freezing, but the coldest I've ever been was in the wet jungle. That day was so dismal that I felt all alone and extremely isolated. I couldn't stand it.

"There was no way to go back, but the thought of sitting another day in a canoe full of water was more than I could bear. My clothes and body would be drenched the entire day.

"It was bad enough that *I* would be painfully cold and wet. What about little Valerie? She would experience the same misery."

But God did not exempt them from this ordeal.

"I still had to go out in the rain and have my little daughter with me in the bottom of the canoe. I still had to return to that lonely place in the jungle."

Then the Lord brought to the new widow's mind the words of Jesus to His disciples when He was leaving them and they were in despair: "I am with you always, even to the end of the world (Matthew 28:20)."

On this dark, bleak day, remembering Jesus' words transformed Elisabeth's perspective of the situation.

What changed?

"Jesus Christ was *there* in the canoe with Valerie and me. He said to me, 'I have loved you with an everlasting love (Jeremiah 31:3).' I knew I was not alone."

Young Valerie and her mother, Elisabeth, relaxing in 1960.

Survive? Impossible!

Widowed with an infant,
how could she go on living?

BY JEANETTE CHAFFEE

WHEN AUCA INDIANS KILLED HER HUSBAND, ELISABETH Elliot was suddenly left alone to raise Valerie, their ten-month-old. "This was a terrible time for me. I was sure it was the *one thing* that I could never survive."

Yet despite the heartache of the tragedy, she realized that the Lord had a plan. "The God who engineers the universe had good things in mind in the death of my husband."

Over the years, she has met hundreds whose lives have been transformed by Jim's testimony.

"On one occasion, I met a young detective in Belfast. His job took him every day into the war zone. He told me that Jim Elliot's biography, *Shadow of the Almighty*, inspired him to know that life came out of death."

Elisabeth points out that death turning into life is a principle of nature. "There is no such thing as life that doesn't come out of death in some form. When we eat a piece of meat, something had to die. When we eat vegetables and fruits, things are dying. And there wouldn't be a peach tree if a peach stone hadn't fallen into the ground and died."

Jesus articulated this principle in the book of John: "Unless a kernel of wheat falls to the ground and dies, it remains only a single seed. But if it dies, it produces many seeds (12:24)."

Just like Elisabeth's husband. She didn't think she could survive Jim's death, but God showed her a way. "I have utmost confidence that God *does* know what He's doing. I trust Him."

The "Eternal Yes" to me will
be worth it in the end. To me,
it's an acceptance of His love.
If He loved me enough to die
for me, then He's someone
I can trust. Even if I don't
understand what's happening,
even if I don't like it, I'll take
it. I say, "Yes Lord!" I believe,
in the end, it will mean joy.

Elisabeth Elliot

My Mother's Heartaches and Joys

Wasn't it bad enough having her first husband die?

BY JEANETTE CHAFFEE

VALERIE ELLIOT DESCRIBES THE FOUNDATION OF HER mother's faith and life in the simplest of terms: "Elisabeth [Elliot] believed what her parents had taught her about Jesus."

HOUSE GUESTS CHANGE ELISABETH'S LIFE

"IN 1934, when my mother was eight years old," Valerie says, "missionaries to China visited their home in Pennsylvania. She told me that this made a deep impression. The woman, Betty Scott Stam, gave Elisabeth a special prayer:

> Lord, I give up all my own plans and purposes, all my own desires and hopes, and accept Thy will for my life.

I give myself, my life, my all, utterly to Thee to be Thine forever. Fill me and seal me with Thy Holy Spirit, use me as Thou wilt, send me where Thou wilt, work out Thy whole will in my life at any cost, now and forever.

The answer to this prayer would cost John and Betty Stam their lives. That December, they were beheaded by the Communists in China.

Little Elisabeth had planned to be a surgeon. However, at age twelve, God called her to the mission field. She decided this meant she would become a medical missionary. Elisabeth put Betty's words in her Bible and prayed them frequently. Valerie says fondly, "Mother quoted from the prayer whenever she spoke."

FIRST LOVE

VALERIE'S mother, Elisabeth (Howard), attended Wheaton College. There she met fellow student Jim Elliot from Portland, Oregon. He

The Howard family in 1948. Elisabeth is fourth from the left.

was on the wrestling team and was popular because he was fun-loving. He was keenly intelligent — a student of Greek and the Bible.

Jim and Elisabeth, from her personal scrapbook.

Elisabeth and Jim went on long walks together, but didn't have many "dates." Instead, they enjoyed each other's company while sipping Cokes at the snack shop.

They also sang, did mock voice-overs, and hilarious comedic impressions—accents and imitations of funny voices. They had a good time being creative. Although the couple loved having fun, both were serious students.

Valerie's parents fell deeply in love, but Jim was cautious. "Mother said Dad did not have the 'green light' from the Lord to marry her."

They would wait five years.

During this time, Jim heard an elderly missionary speak about the primitive and violent Auca Indians. The man had traveled to Ecuador, but all attempts to contact the natives had failed, as they were extremely hostile to outsiders.

Jim was moved by the plight of the Auca. He began a regular prayer routine. He wondered, "Why don't *I* go talk to them?" and soon he was making plans to go to Ecuador.

NOTHING BUT LOSS

JIM and his friend, Pete Fleming, sailed to Ecuador and arrived in February 1952. Elisabeth came later on a mission to minister to the local Colorado Indians. Joining her was Dorothy, another linguist.

Jim in Oakland, California.

In Quito, the women moved into their own place near the men. The group met frequently for Spanish lessons and they ate meals together.

Jim and Elisabeth continued their slow romance. They took walks in the nearby pastures, rode the bus together to the post office, had fun watching sunrises, and practiced speaking their Spanish to anyone who would listen. Though in love, they were primarily concerned about following God's plan.

Six months later, the women left for their assigned village, San Miguel de los Colorados. Getting there was an adventure: hours in the bumpy bed of a truck and then even more on horseback.

Jim headed to the Eastern Ecuador jungles to work with the Quichua Indians. Since he was on the other side of the Andes, Elisabeth knew it would be months until they saw each other again. They planned to write letters weekly.

Elisabeth and Dorothy found a local who could be an interpreter. They were confident this was God's answer to prayer as Don Macario was the *only* person in the village who was bilingual in both Spanish and Colorado. Most importantly, he was a Christian. He was the key that made communication happen.

Translation work with Don started right away and continued while the women learned the language. Elisabeth spent nine months preparing hundreds of flash cards and language notes with Colorado phonetic sounds and words. She was the first to create its written language.

Elisabeth teaching in the jungle.

One morning in January 1953, Elisabeth was reading her Bible when she heard gunfire—followed by screaming and running. She was horrified to discover that Don had been shot in the forehead while he was clearing land to plant banana trees.

The entire village was devastated.

As Elisabeth tried to come to terms with the murder, she searched for another translator to help with the language work. She couldn't find anyone. A few Indians promised they'd help, but never did.

It was a huge letdown to her. What good was it to be a linguist if she didn't have an expert partner?

Unable to do her translation work, Elisabeth felt lost. Valerie remembers: "Mother thought she was a liability to the Indians. She thought she couldn't offer them anything. They had to feed and take care of her."

No answers came—nothing but questions.

As Elisabeth struggled, she prepared a large suitcase of all the original language materials completed. The plan was to send everything to Quito for duplication. Some fellow missionaries hand-carried the priceless case. A few days later Elisabeth was stunned to learn that her only copies of the three-by-five-inch cards and linguistic notes had all been stolen.

Why did the Lord allow this? She prayed: *Lord, how can I trust You when all my work is gone?*

Despite these trials, Valerie insists her mother always lived by faith. "She was not a feelings-oriented person. Mother was a firm believer in living by principles, not emotions. She didn't want people to feel sorry for her or to draw attention to herself."

Across the Andes, Jim was facing his own tragedy at the Missionary Aviation Fellowship community where he lived. He repaired old buildings, built two new ones, and spent months making boards by hand from raw timber. He planned to use this lumber for new construction, but a sudden flood destroyed the entire village. All his work was for nothing.

Flood, theft, and murder: a total loss of everything. What did Elisabeth and Jim have to show for their first year on the mission field?

Is this the cost of obedience? Elisabeth wondered.

God answered with a question: Will you trust Me even though these things have happened?

THE DELIGHTFUL SURPRISE

THE night of January 29, 1953, Elisabeth heard a horse approaching. She grabbed a lantern and hurried outside. Someone handed her a telegram. *A telegram?* she thought. *What terrible thing happened?*

To her relief nothing was wrong. The message was from Jim—he was in Quito and wanted her to visit.

Delighted, she immediately prepared to go. As she packed, she wondered about their relationship. Would they ever marry? Though she knew they deeply loved each other, their commitment to Christ came first. He'd written in her college yearbook: "Take your share of suffering… as Christ's soldier and do not let yourself become tied up with the affairs of this life (2 Timothy 2:3–5)."

Their reunion in Quito was joyous. Jim told her that the Lord was releasing him from singleness. He was ready to marry her. Elisabeth couldn't have been happier. She prayed for guidance... and said "Yes!"

After waiting nearly five years, she was more than ready.

They married on October 8, 1953 and moved to Arajuno. It was a difficult first six months. They lived in a leaking tent, and soon both of them contracted hepatitis.

However, they "were so much in love," says Valerie, "that they didn't think about their troubles."

MORE GRIEF

FOR the next two years, Jim and Elisabeth worked with the Quichua Indians. She learned the language and taught the Bible. In early 1955 the couple was delighted with the birth of Valerie.

"Pilipinto watched the ground going backwards."

Sketch of Valerie being carried by a Quichua Indian. Her nickname was "Pilipinto" (butterfly).

During this time Jim still felt his burden for the Auca. He had never forgotten their plight. He and several other missionaries began work on Operation Auca, an attempt to communicate with the remote and inhospitable Stone Age people.

Sadly, on January 8, 1956, those efforts ended with death.

The people Jim had been praying for since his college days, had killed him.

Valerie explains, "My mother's marriage of twenty-seven months suddenly ended when Dad, along with four colleagues, were speared to death." (See "Speared: Betrayed by New Friends" on page 51.)

Through her grief, Elisabeth wrote a book about the death of the missionaries. *Through Gates of Splendor* became a best-seller. Her follow-up a year later, *Shadow of the Almighty,* was a biography of her husband.

GOD HAD A PLAN

YEARS earlier, an Auca girl, Dayuma, had fled the violent tribe after her father was murdered. Eventually she was befriended by missionary Rachel Saint and became the first Auca convert. In 1958, Dayuma learned that her mother wanted to see her. After visiting home for the first time in many years, Dayuma invited Rachel and Elisabeth to come live with the Auca.

This began the *first* peaceful contact with the savage tribe. Dayuma was influential and helped the Americans unlock the language. Elisabeth was given an Auca name, *Gikari,* which means "woodpecker." Over time, many Auca accepted Jesus. The generation that had killed the five men said they would no longer kill — and they haven't.

Elisabeth and young Valerie lived there for two years. After several more years working with the Quichua Indians, they moved to the United States for Valerie to have an American education.

A DIFFERENT WAY OF LIFE

AS a young woman growing up without a dad, Valerie could relate to her mother's heartaches.

"I'm sure that for many years her greatest sorrow was losing Jim. They thought they'd be on the mission field all their lives and would have four children. Instead, they only had one—me. Mother never dreamed that my dad would be killed."

After four years back in the States, Elisabeth met Addison Leitch. He taught at Gordon Conwell Theological Seminary. Her heart was moved and a year later, they married. She and her daughter relocated to Massachusetts.

"The heartache of my dad's absence transformed into love for a wonderful, brilliant, funny man, who was also a great writer and thinker." For thirteen-year-old Valerie, having a father was a blessing. She loved Addison's humor and his storytelling.

Sadly, just five years later he passed away from cancer. Valerie was eighteen when he died. She understood her mother's terrible sorrow and remembers her praying, "Lord, how could you take away the second husband? It was bad enough losing one—but why two?"

Elisabeth calculated that despite two marriages, she'd

Three generations: Elisabeth, with her daughter Valerie, and two of her grandchildren.

been single more years than married. But soon the Lord provided a third husband: Lars Gren, a hospital chaplain.

With her in high demand around the country as an author and speaker, Lars took care of the details of travel and helped sell her various books. She also hosted a radio program called *Gateway to Joy*.

They've enjoyed a wonderful life together for over thirty-five years.

GRANDCHILDREN

VALERIE attended Wheaton College, where her father and mother had met and fallen in love. After graduating, she married a pastor, Walter Shepard. They had eight children who adored their grandparents.

"Lars has a great sense of humor," granddaughter Christiana says.

Another granddaughter and namesake, Elisabeth, describes special visits such as going to *The 700 Club*.

"Lars and Granny liked to take us grandchildren with them on trips and outings. It was Gramps who taught me how to enjoy fine dining, which silverware to use, and in what order. Being in a large family meant that going out to eat was a real treat. Thanks to

Elisabeth and Lars in 2006.

Granny and Gramps, I got to do this at least once a year, 'on their dime,' as Gramps put it."

INSPIRED BY MY MOTHER

VALERIE is impressed by her mother's sense of faith despite all the heartaches. "She focuses on knowing the Lord, being faithful to Him, and answering God's question: 'Will you trust me—even though you don't understand?'"

Elisabeth loves Isaiah 43. "When you walk through the fire, you shall not be burned, nor shall the flame scorch you. For I am the Lord your God (verses 2-3)."

"This helped her not to be afraid after my dad was killed," Valerie remembers. "Mother constantly keeps her eyes on Jesus, rather than on her circumstances. She always concentrates on the Scriptures. I recall her saying: 'It's not what I could do. I am to be faithful. I am to be a good steward. I am to *know* Him. I'm not to focus on saving people, but knowing the Lord.'

"She didn't like it when people would talk about how many souls they had saved. Rather, 'We are to be witnesses. We know and believe that He is the Lord (Isaiah 43:10).'"

An important lesson Valerie learned is not putting too much emphasis on feelings. "Mother said, 'It's not how I felt, but what I knew the Lord showed me in the Word—*no matter what.*'"

Today Valerie strives to live her life by faith. She follows Abraham as an example. "His obedience made him righteous. He never talked about his emotions. There's nothing in the Bible about what he felt or what was going on in his heart. Abraham believed God."

So does Valerie.

KEN MEDEMA

Although blind from birth, **KEN MEDEMA** was drawn to music early in life. He studied music at Michigan State University and later worked as a music therapist. In 1985, he founded Brier Patch Music, a recording, publishing, and booking company. He has appeared as a singer and pianist for presidents of the United States, at the National Speakers Association, on the *Hour of Power*, and at fundraisers for Habitat for Humanity. Ken continues performing at over two hundred events per year.

He and his wife, Jane, have been married since 1965. They have grown children, Aaron and Rachel, and two grand-children. Ken and Jane proudly call the San Francisco area home.

*It is a terrible thing to see and
have no vision... The only
thing worse than being blind
is having sight but not seeing.*

Helen Keller

A Different Way of Seeing

Born blind, yet he performs before presidents

BY JEANETTE CHAFFEE

WHEN HE WAS A CHILD, KEN MEDEMA HARBORED DEEP resentment about being born blind. "Other kids did not want to play or be with me. I felt ugly and graceless. I wasn't able to play sports. I didn't receive positive reinforcement from other kids." Throughout his public school days, he struggled to cope.

Then he faced the problem of dating. "I couldn't ask girls out on dates. After all, since I couldn't drive, did I want to tell my date that my mother would drive us around?"

As a result, Ken was bored and lonely, and stayed in the house by himself. At the age of eleven he made a life-changing decision to start practicing the piano and singing three to four hours a day. His parents and teachers offered him many positive affirmations.

"They believed in me. They let me know that I would be a fine performer and travel the world. They continued encouraging me to be all that I could be. And I believed them!

"I knew that if I could find the right niche, I could do whatever I wanted to do. I always kept in mind, "I can do all things through Christ who strengthens me (Philippians 4:13).'"

He had confidence that someday he would be Leonard Bernstein on the piano.

Life became much easier for Ken after high school. At Michigan State University he met a fellow music student, Jane. They had the same piano instructor. Her father was a Baptist pastor.

One day, while working on an arrangement of the song "When I Fall In Love" — not what he was supposed to be practicing, of course — Jane stopped by and he played the song for her.

She said, "I hate you."

"Why?" he asked.

"Because you make me cry."

"Then let me buy you some coffee to say I'm sorry for making you cry," Ken responded.

The couple immediately went out. "We sat at the coffee shop almost the whole day talking about religion, philosophy, our life mission, music, travel, parents, history, and when we were through, I knew that something magical had happened."

Ken began going to church with Jane — he hadn't been to church during his first year of college.

"It was our meeting that brought me back to faith. Although I was raised in a Christian family, I did not surrender to Christ until I was a student in college. Then my life was transformed."

His peers had also changed. Winning a basketball game, dating a beauty queen, and being popular weren't as important — being a fine musician was now respected.

After college, Ken went on to a fantastic career as a musician. Soon he was performing two hundred times a year — something he's continued to do for over thirty years — and eventually playing before President Jimmy Carter in 1974 and at President Bill Clinton's Inauguration Eve Prayer Service in 1993.

Ken continued to fall in love with Jesus. Psalm 42:1-2 became one of his favorite verses. "As the deer pants for the water brooks, so my heart pants for You, O God. My soul thirsts for God, for the living God."

Still, a nagging problem plagued him.

He had spent his life trying to prove himself through his music. Ken did things that *seemed* to have the right motivation, but he knew the truth.

His deep insecurities made him seek approval and he designed his concerts in search of acceptance. He admits:

"I wrote songs that made people cry because of the deep meaning in the music. I had to make sure everyone would like me so I didn't say what I felt. I was a chameleon. I wanted to make people believe that I was cool."

Despite a successful career, Ken's need for affirmation grew deeper and deeper — much like the insatiable need of an alcoholic.

In his forties, with support from his friends and his wife, Ken made a conscious decision to become emotionally honest. It was a long process.

Ken performing at the piano.

"I realized how people-pleasing was ruining my life and preventing me from being myself. I didn't need this in my life anymore.

"I believe this is a disease in religious circles. For example, a Christian woman may feel she needs to be perfect in her appearance all the time, perfect at church, perfect as a wife and mother. She may run herself into the ground being Miss Perfect."

Ken realized how many people—like himself—spend their entire adult lives acting like someone they can never be.

"Nice is nice, but honest is better." He could no longer just be the sweet guy. He had to be himself.

"Much to my surprise, I got more genuine respect from others when I showed my real true self."

Having lived with feelings of loneliness and separation, Ken has empathy for people who experience political oppression, physical disabilities, or mental problems—such as San Francisco's homeless population. The lyrics in many of his songs reflect this passion. He's also worked as a music therapist, allowing the troubled to express themselves through music.

Does Ken wish he could see?

He would love to see Jane. Snowflakes falling. Lake Michigan. Printed music. Leaves on trees. Canyons.

However, he has his own way of seeing the world: singing *and* playing. "I cannot ever separate the two; they belong together for me."

Similar to his indivisible relationship with Jesus.

He is finally whole.

SHIRLEY DOBSON

SHIRLEY DOBSON has been honored with numerous awards, including Christian Woman of the Year, Church-woman of the Year, Full-Time Homemaker of the Year, and W.A. Shirley Chriswell Lifetime Christian Citizenship Award. She was invited to the White House by President Ronald Reagan for a Christian Women's Leadership Conference in 1988. She has received four honorary doctorates and is chair of the National Day of Prayer Task Force.

Her husband, Dr. James Dobson, is founder and president of the Family Talk radio program. They have grown children, Ryan and Danae. Shirley is delighted that her grandchildren, Lincoln and Luci, live just ten minutes away in Colorado Springs.

There are far, far better
things ahead than any
we leave behind.

C. S. Lewis

Where God Guides . . . God Provides

What good could possibly come from leaving their beloved home of thirty years?

BY JEANETTE CHAFFEE

SHIRLEY DOBSON SAID THAT ONE OF THE MOST DIFFICULT challenges she has experienced was moving from Southern California to Colorado in 1991. Having been the daughter of an alcoholic father, she found her security in the stability of her home and marriage, and, of course, in her dependence on Jesus Christ. The Dobsons had lived in the same house for nineteen years, attended the same church for three decades, and were surrounded by dozens of friends they had known and loved since college. Their grown children lived close by, as did her mother and stepfather. Shirley's great desire was to remain in this secure nest.

Then the Focus on the Family board of directors decided that it was time to move the ministry to Colorado. Property in the Golden State was too expensive for their growing organization, and California was taxing them mercilessly, even as a nonprofit organization. Colorado offered no taxes for the life of the ministry, and pristine land was one dollar per square foot. Clearly, it was wise to move, so the executives loaded seventy-five semitrailer trucks and headed east.

Dr. Dobson was understanding of his wife's reluctance to move, but he felt God's call. He joked that Shirley left drag marks from California all across the Rockies.

Shirley knew her responsibility was to follow her husband, wherever he felt led to go. They resettled in a modest townhouse which was nothing like the Cape Cod home they had in California. Their new abode, "The Springs," looked like a ski lodge instead of a traditional house with a manicured yard. However, that wasn't what troubled Shirley. She missed the friends and loved ones she had left behind.

She did her best to be cheerful and supportive to her husband during their first few months in Colorado Springs, but she still longed for the joy she had known during their thirty-one years in California. One day, she was getting dressed and putting on her makeup when it seemed as though the Lord spoke to her spirit.

"Shirley, I'm not concerned about your *happiness*. I am concerned that you are in My will. And it is My will that you be in Colorado Springs."

At that moment, she yielded fully and irrevocably to her circumstances. She said, "All right, Lord. I would rather be in Your will than to be happy."

From that moment to this, Shirley has had perfect peace about her circumstances. She had been asked to serve as chair of the National Day of Prayer Task Force, and she's poured her life into that responsibility for over twenty years. Certainly she could have held that post while in California, but the pieces came together in a way that would not have occurred "at home."

Soon her son, Ryan, and his wife, Laura, came to Colorado. They now live with two precious grandchildren only ten minutes away. Her daughter, Danae, comes to Colorado frequently, and she sees her family as often as when they were in California. The friends they had there have all moved, and her parents have gone on to be with the Lord. Life was destined to change even if they had stayed in their nest.

Shirley likens her situation to that of Abraham and Sarah in the Bible. Jehovah called them to leave their family and friends and journey to an unknown land, and no doubt Sarah fretted about the move.

What motivates Shirley to share her story is the hope that it will encourage those who are dissatisfied with their state of life. She offers these words of advice: "Where God guides... God will provide." It is better to be in His will than to have everything your heart desires. Yielding to His gentle leading is *always* the right thing to do, even when it is difficult.

Stated another way, someone has written, "Let go, and let God." That is exactly what Shirley did. And she has never regretted yielding to Him.

Shirley and Dr. Dobson in Colorado.

DONNIE DEE

A native of Kansas City, **DONNIE DEE** played both football and basketball in high school. He continued to play football in college at the University of Tulsa and as a tight end for the Indianapolis Colts from 1988 to 1990. Donnie's great love for professional sports came from his father's American Basketball Association career, playing with the Pacers and being a member of Team USA for the 1968 Olympics basketball team, winning gold in Mexico City. After leaving the NFL, Donnie began to work with Fellowship of Christian Athletes (FCA) in Denver and later in San Diego. He grew FCA's ministry in Southern California from one volunteer to thirty staff members. In August of 2009, Donnie became the executive director and chief operating officer of FCA, the largest sports ministry in the world. He has been affiliated with them for twenty-four years. He and his wife, Jackie, have two adult children and call San Diego home.

Everyone has the power for greatness. Not for fame, but greatness. Because greatness is determined by service.

Dr. Martin Luther King

Journey From a Broken Home to the NFL

After living with an alcoholic gold medalist, this NFL player gets a new boss

BY JEANETTE CHAFFEE

"T HERE IS NO QUESTION THAT BEING FROM A BROKEN HOME and having an alcoholic father were the most difficult things I've ever been through," Donnie Dee says. "They were life-changers for me. They were also the most shaping times of my life. My family was definitely a dysfunctional family."

He grew up in a high-achieving and competitive family. His father played basketball with the Pacers and was selected to be on Team USA in the Mexico City Olympics. They beat the Czechs and won the gold medal. But in spite of being raised in the home of a successful professional athlete, an unfulfilled desire haunted Donnie's soul.

His father was the local kid who made it big in both the ABA (American Basketball Association) and the Olympics, and being a businessman, owning a couple of restaurants in Kansas City and coaching Little League baseball filled his time.

"Dad was never abusive or neglectful; he just wasn't the dad I longed to have. He was a good and gentle man, but not a Christian. Dad failed as a husband. He failed, in some ways, as a father."

Donnie realized he had some tough decisions to make. What kind of person did he want to become? What kind of dad and husband did he want to be?"

He admits his dad was a better father than his grandfather had been. Still, Donnie ached for a deeper relationship. "He wasn't nearly the kind of dad I wanted. I longed for a dad who was involved with me. I wanted more of his time. I wanted to know that he loved me. I wanted him to be proud of me.

"There were times when he said these things to me." But Donnie always wanted more. "I probably tell my kids 'I love you' and 'I'm proud of you' more than most people do because I didn't get to hear them as much as I wanted.

"Dad also wasn't affectionate or emotionally connected. I've only seen him cry once in his life—when he heard that his father had died."

Donnie was the oldest child, followed by Stephen, Lisa, and Mike—four kids in five years. "Mom's joke was that she was already pregnant again before she came home from the hospital!" It was, unfortunately, never "just Dad and me."

His mother was hardworking and ambitious. "She was driven and excelled at everything, a self-made woman. Mom went from not finishing high school to becoming the CEO of the Kansas City Convention Center."

A great tragedy struck her at the age of thirteen. "Mom's father was a policeman in Kansas City. One night, while he was off duty, he intervened in a bar fight. One of the disgruntled fighters went out to his truck, returned with a shotgun, and killed her dad. As a result, Mom didn't get to graduate from high school. She was the second oldest (her brother had already left home), and she took care of her two younger siblings."

He thinks about what his mom experienced, in her childhood and later with her own family. She showed a lot of love and always gave the children encouragement and direction. "What Mom did that was so significant was to keep the family together. Next to the Lord, she was the single biggest reason we're all in a good place today. It was her love and leadership in our family."

But Dad was still the patriarch of the household — because of his size and because of what he had accomplished. The family looked up to him.

However, someone can be a figurehead without taking the authority to be the leader. This is true of sports, business, and family.

"Dad had the right to be the leader, but he never assumed that God-given responsibility, because he wasn't a Christian. He never took the opportunity that he had to be more than a figurehead.

The Dee family: Jackie, Johnny, Jenny, and Donnie in 2011.

His alcoholic behaviors fostered terrible dysfunction and chaos for the family.

"Alcohol allowed Dad to escape from the daily pressures of life and having to make decisions. He didn't accept responsibilities and remained disconnected from the issues at hand. He would put responsibilities back on Mom or blame us kids."

Donnie realized that while his mother was focused on family life, his dad was only concerned about his alcohol.

"Beer or other liquor was *the* most important thing in Dad's life. Being a big man, he held his liquor. No DUIs. No stupors. No falling unconscious on the floor. No violence."

Even today his dad drinks, starting at one o'clock and continuing until bedtime. "He likes who he is when he's drinking. He looks forward to it. He can't imagine life without it. It's sad."

Donnie now has a better feel for what makes his dad tick, though he wishes his dad had loved Jesus and been a better parent. "He's a great guy to drink with. He's a great guy on the court. He's a great teammate in competitive sports. But he's a hard guy to live with."

One day he asked his dad, "When are you going to stop drinking?" His dad replied, "Then what would I do?"

When Donnie was in eighth grade, his parents divorced. Lisa went to live with her mom; the three boys lived with their dad. Arguing and fighting seemed normal to Donnie because he didn't know anything different. Nearly all his friends came from broken homes.

"We four kids were all confused about the family, marriage, love, and commitment. Our worlds were rocked. Because of our dysfunction, we rallied and became close. We still are. We always enjoy seeing each other."

Donnie took the breakup the hardest. He internalized his doubts and wondered, *What did I do – or didn't I do – that made them divorce?*

"Things were definitely weird after the split. We all had to get into the rhythm of a new way of life. I longed for my family to be together. For two years I kept asking my parents, 'When are you coming home?' and 'When are you two getting back together?' Eventually, I got it: they wouldn't. It wasn't going to happen. I was the last one to accept it was over."

As an adult, Donnie knows how love takes effort and sacrifice. "The thing I longed for was the same thing my mom craved. As an eighth grader, I didn't understand marriage and relationships. Now I'm aware that marriage takes hard work."

There were some good times. The family took fishing trips at their lake home. There was "Basketball 101" when he was thirteen. All week he praticed shooting at an old hoop with a ripped net. Then he asked his dad to play him.

"Dad didn't even warm up. Of course, he could have beaten me if he had wanted to—just with his size alone. But he didn't win. I beat him! Even to this day it's one of my greatest memories."

He loved coming straight home after his high school basketball games. Since his folks were divorced, that meant time with Dad. Donnie always had to initiate the conversation. "Dad would be drinking a beer, and we'd talk about the game, what I did well and what I could improve on."

Though his dad was a world-class athlete, Donnie was amazed and relieved that there was never any pressure to play sports. "No matter how many points I scored—even if only ten—Dad would tell me: 'Good job, Donnie. I'm proud of you and how you played.'

"As a sixteen-, seventeen-, eighteen-year-old, hearing this meant the world to me." He has adopted this same style with his teenagers.

Donnie had a lifelong dream of playing in the National Football League. It came closer to reality when he received a football scholarship to the University of Tulsa. What more could he possibly desire? He lived for sports—it was always his god. "All I wanted to do was play football and professional sports like my father."

His dream lasted two weeks.

Colliding with a linebacker's helmet, he broke his thumb and required surgery. In a fleeting moment—*whoosh*—sports and the NFL evaporated. Donnie's fantasy became a nightmare, filled with dark, plaguing questions. *Will I recover? What if I can't play?*

Donnie, playing for the Indianapolis Colts.

While he was recuperating, several teammates who were members of the Fellowship of Christian Athletes (FCA) extended kindness to him. One evening they came to his dorm room and talked with him about Jesus Christ.

As they spoke, he experienced flashbacks of going to church in his childhood. "We *always* went on Easter and Christmas because those are the big holidays, and that's what good religious people did!"

His memories of church were crystal clear:

Boring. "I didn't understand anything about a relationship. I just remember seeing a picture of a man hanging on a cross."

A waste of time. "I didn't want to spend my life sitting in a building listening to something I didn't understand."

Repetitive. "Church services were a tedious routine — and teenagers are anything *but* routine!"

These memories revived secret questions he had pondered as a child. *What does God want from me? What is God like? Why was I created? What's with the guy hanging on that cross?*

It had been years since he'd thought of those questions. What good were they?

Now, with his athletic hopes fading and his anxieties growing, he listened to his teammates. "All those thoughts connected when these guys told me about Jesus. When I first heard the message of the Son of God dying on the cross for my sins, my eyes were opened to the light.

"As a child, I had always looked at God as Santa Claus. After all, you go to Santa Claus when you need stuff. My prayers, even as a little kid, were about me and not about God, because I didn't know anything about Him.

"I had never read the Bible in my life. I never knew Jesus died for me. I didn't know anybody who claimed to be a Christ-follower."

His teammates kept talking with him in that Tulsa dorm room. "Jesus promises, in Revelation 3:20: 'Look! I have been standing at the door, and I am constantly knocking. If anyone hears Me calling him and opens the door, I will come in and fellowship with him and he with Me.'"

They explained that his heart was a door, and if he opened it, Jesus would come in and be with him. It was up to him to open the door because Jesus wouldn't kick it in.

This picture was significant to Donnie.

"I clearly understood the gospel that night and it was one of the things that led to my decision. Breaking my thumb and having

Donnie speaking at a Fellowship of Christian Athletes event.

surgery were parts of the process that made me realize there had to be something more besides football."

He prayed: "I have made other things the boss of my life. Now I want You, Lord Jesus, to be the new boss of my life. I know You have to be the most important thing."

His teammates began high-fiving and hugging him. "This is the decision that will change your life," they promised.

Donnie agrees. "I can look back on this now and say they were absolutely right!"

Then the guys explained it was time to learn and understand God's Word. They started regularly teaching him about Jesus and the Bible. He was excited about his future. "I was informed, enlightened, and part of God's family."

He marveled, *How could I have gone to church for eighteen years and never heard of anything so remarkable?*

"When playing football switched roles with God, He had to become the most important thing in my life. God gave me the desires of my heart. That was to play college and professional football."

After Donnie retired from professional football in 1990, he began working for FCA and today is their executive director and chief operating officer.

He is overwhelmed with gratitude.

"I can say this has never been about being a job. It's always an opportunity to say thanks. Every day I serve is out of a grateful heart. I could work for this organization for a hundred years and never give back what I have gotten."

MARILEE PIERCE DUNKER

MARILEE (PIERCE) DUNKER is the second daughter of Bob Pierce, founder of World Vision and Samaritan's Purse. Among her many accomplishments, Marilee cohosted *Focus on the Family* and had her own radio talk show. She has written four books, including her family's story, *Man of Vision*. For the past thirteen years, Marilee has traveled the world for World Vision as a speaker and advocate for women and children. She is finishing her fifth book, *The Audacity of Faith*.

Let my heart be broken
with the things that
break the heart of God.

Dr. Bob Pierce

Finishing Well

The four-year-old girl is asked
to sing before thousands

BY JEANETTE CHAFFEE

MARILEE PIERCE'S SINGING DEBUT IN 1954 WAS AT HER father's evangelistic meeting at the Pasadena Civic Auditorium. Dr. Bob Pierce and his special guest, Dale Evans, had drawn a capacity crowd.

The four-year-old didn't feel nervous until her father walked her to the microphone and the music began to play. Taking a deep breath, she opened her mouth and was relieved to hear the song, "There is a Wonderful Guest at Our House," come out in a strong, clear voice.

As Marilee confidently finished the first verse, the audience burst into applause. Though there was a second verse to sing, she was so startled she left the stage. After all, if the audience was clapping, the song must be over, right?

"I rushed into my mother's arms, overwhelmed with an unfamiliar feeling of disappointment," Marilee recalls.

"Later, my father asked me a question that I have never forgotten: *'Why didn't you finish?'*

"God has often reminded me of that night when I have been tempted to leave other 'songs' unfinished... a book, a teaching, or a new friendship I should nurture. I have come to appreciate the guiding truth that my father understood so well."

The apostle Paul said it best in Philippians 3:13-14: "Forgetting what lies behind and reaching forward to what lies ahead, I press on toward the goal for the prize of the upward call of God in Christ Jesus."

Marilee continues to live by the truth of her father's question. "It doesn't matter how you begin. It's how you finish that counts."

World Vision founder Dr. Bob Pierce with his daughter, Marilee, in 1954, at the Civic Auditorium in Pasadena, California.

JERRY & SUSANNE MCCLAIN

JERRY AND SUSANNE MCCLAIN were child stars. Susanne began singing when she could talk. At age four, Jerry sang on his father's weekly radio show. Their fast, catapulting successes arrived during their college days at UCLA, where they graduated. It was there that they met Dr. Bill Bright and Hal Lindsey. In the following years, they performed with stars like Phyllis Diller, the Smothers Brothers, Red Skeleton, and Johnny Mathis. They appeared on John Davidson's *Kraft Summer Music Hall* and Dick Clark's *American Bandstand*. Anita Kerr contracted to manage their dream band, Brother Love. From 1963 to 1979, their names appeared on marquees in Las Vegas, Reno, and Miami.

Folks worldwide heard the couple singing "Happy Days," the catchy theme song to the TV show of the same name. *Happy Days* aired weekly on television from 1974 to 1984, offering a romanticized vision of American life in the mid-1950s. America fell in love with the hit ABC sitcom, which included guest appearances with celebrities such as Robin Williams (appearing as Mork from *Mork and Mindy*), Dr. Joyce Brothers (helping Fonzie's depressed dog), and John Hart (*The Lone Ranger*). The song "Happy Days" was number one on the *Billboard* charts in 1976-1977.

The McClains have attended Church on the Way in Van Nuys, California, since it was founded with one hundred members. They have an adult son, Jarret, and reside in North Hollywood, a few blocks from Henry "The Fonz" Winkler.

Saturday, What a day
Rockin' all week with you
These Happy Days are
yours and mine.

Lyrics and Music by
Fox and Gimbel

Recorded and sung by
Pratt, McClain, and others

Not Always Happy Days

Overnight, a Hollywood couple goes from having it all to losing it all

BY JEANETTE CHAFFEE

OTH JERRY AND SUSANNE MCCLAIN SANG AND PERFORMED
from their earliest childhood. At age four, Jerry sang on his
father's radio show. Susanne talks about how "my twin
sister and I played violin, sang, and danced. By tenth grade we
were singing for school."

SPRING SING

UCLA'S largest event was the annual Spring Sing. In 1964, one day
before auditions, Jerry and some fraternity brothers decided they
should try out. Jerry knew talented twin sisters who sang and
danced and thought they would be a plus for their show. (Jerry
had briefly dated Susanne, the blond.) He headed over to the Tri
Delta sorority to ask the sisters to join. They agreed.

Hastily, the members chose a song and scribbled barely-known
lyrics on the palms of their hands. Minutes before showtime, they

realized they didn't even have a name for the group—and decided to call themselves The Lively Set. Their audition was successful, and they were scheduled to perform in the finals at the Hollywood Bowl.

While rehearsing for the big event, Jerry realized that Susanne was the perfect woman for him. They fell in love, and marriage seemed inevitable.

However, Jerry was in a quandary. He had given his life to Jesus at the age of ten. Susanne, on the other hand, belonged to a church, sang in the choir, and was confirmed and baptized, but she did not *personally* know Jesus.

Though it shattered his heart, Jerry broke up with her. He told her, "You know *of* the Lord, but you don't *know* the Lord." He felt God didn't want him to marry someone who wasn't a Christian, just as the Scriptures say not to be "unequally yoked (2 Corinthians 6:14)." He wanted God's plan for his life—exclusively.

He arranged for Susanne to meet with Hal Lindsey's wife, Jan. Jan invited Susanne to her home. She explained that "intellectual religion"—doing good works, knowing the right prayers, being baptized, and going to church—was not the same thing as knowing Jesus *personally*. Susanne needed to ask Christ to forgive her sins and accept Him into her heart as her Savior and Lord.

Jerry remembers Susanne's excited call. "She said, 'I have Someone in my heart!'"

With the romance back on and graduation looming, the two focused their attention on Spring Sing at the Hollywood Bowl. It must have worked because the celebrity judges, Randy Sparks (of The New Christy Minstrels) and Johnny Mercer, declared The Lively Set the grand prize winners!

FAME AND FORTUNE

SUCH recognition from the well-known judges instantly catapulted the group of seven performers—now renamed The American

Scene, into show business. Greg Garrison, the producer of *The Dean Martin Show*, called with an offer to tape in February. He and Dean had watched the musical group open for Rowan & Martin and loved what they saw.

Many offers followed, resulting in a regular circuit of business in Lake Tahoe, Las Vegas, Reno, and Miami.

"We performed in great night clubs and stayed in posh hotel rooms," Susanne says. "It was thrilling for us, since we were barely twenty and twenty-one years old, to see our names in marquee lights at the Riviera!"

During the summer of 1966, Bob Banner, producer of *The Carol Burnett Show*, wanted to feature new, young talent. John Davidson hosted *The Kraft Summer Music Hall*, which showcased musical variety and ran for over three months. Every week The American Scene sang and danced their way into the hearts of millions.

Joining them were other unknown young performers, including comedians Richard Pryor and George Carlin, along with Flip Wilson, Gary Lewis, and the Everly Brothers.

In the summer of 1966, Campus Crusade founder Dr. Bill Bright called Jerry and Susanne. "Will you come to our headquarters and assist the musical touring group [The New Folk Singers] with choreography?"

Jerry and Susanne were ecstatic.

There they met a brilliant musician named Michael Omartian. This marked the beginning of a lifelong friendship. Michael would become instrumental in making the theme of *Happy Days* a giant hit.

BROTHER LOVE

AFTER going together for four years, Jerry proposed to Susanne on Valentine's Day, 1968. Their good friend, Hal Lindsey (author of *The Late, Great Planet Earth*), married them on August 10.

The next year brought a whirlwind of huge commercials, which, according to Jerry, "grossed us a phenomenal amount of money." The group became the representatives for Doublemint Gum and Standard Oil.

The American Scene was preparing to break up. "We were strong Christians and we loved our UCLA colleagues, but we didn't have the same vision," Jerry recalls. Some wanted to quit show business, and two entered law school. The McClains, on the other hand, wanted the opportunity to share their faith.

In 1969, Jerry and Susanne opened for Johnny Mathis for the month of December. During the final performance, Johnny sang the Neil Diamond gospel song, "Brother Love's Traveling Salvation Show" and the couple immediately knew they had a perfect name for their new group. From that night on, they were Brother Love.

The group also consisted of Michael, his friend Truett Pratt, Susanne's twin sister Diane, and a couple of other musicians.

They used the opportunity to share the Lord with people. They performed their regular show, starting with the "Brother Love" song, and incorporated uplifting songs from the Carpenters, Elton John, and Anne Murray, among others.

"At the end, we did a musical series, written by Michael, and told people that if they wanted to know more about this Jesus, to come see us afterward, back by the bar."

Anita Kerr became the couple's manager. "We told her about Michael. We brought him down from Campus Crusade and mentored him, especially in performing commercials." They also insisted that Columbia Records use Michael.

Jerry will always remember the thrill of Dick Clark introducing them on *American Bandstand* saying, "Jerry McClain, Truett Pratt, and Brother Love."

From Las Vegas to Miami to Seattle, people came. "We prayed with them at the bar, and many are still following the Lord."

The word spread and a lot of Christians came to see them, including Hal Lindsey, who brought his atheist brother-in-law. "He met with me at the back of the bar and accepted the Lord. I told Hal, 'Your brother-in-law just became a born-again Christian.'" Hal was ecstatic since he had prayed many years for him.

One day in 1976, Michael called the McClains and said he had a song that he wanted them to hear. He came over to their house that night and showed them the music and lyrics of "Happy Days."

The next day Jerry went to the studio and sang all the lead parts of the new song. A few days later Brother Love went and recorded all the background music.

"One night we were driving our Corvette to the night club," Susanne recalls. We heard the announcer say, 'Now, here's the latest hit song from the hit show, *Happy Days.*'"

A year later, "Happy Days" was playing on radios all over the country. It would eventually appear worldwide on more than fifty compilation disks.

But tragic events would shatter the lives of the couple who "had it all."

JERRY'S DRUG ADDICTION

IN college, Jerry was clean-cut and had high morals. He was chaplain of his UCLA fraternity. But he acknowledges that "when a person gets too much success, anything can happen."

One day they received an invitation from Warner Brothers for a big celebration party honoring Fleetwood Mac's number-one hit album, *Rumours.* Jerry and Truett attended. Susanne remained at home with their son, Jarret, who wasn't feeling well.

In the suite were Fleetwood Mac, George Harrison, Elton John, Rod Stewart, and several Warner Brothers executives. Jerry remembers thinking: *I can't believe I'm in the same room with these people.*

When folks began snorting cocaine, he became "overcome with the power of being with these famous musicians." Although drugs had never interested him before, he decided to try cocaine just this one time.

"I felt very strongly I could do a little bit and it wouldn't affect me. I had lived at the fraternity and been around a lot of drinking, yet I never drank. I should have known better, because the McClain family was full of highly addictive personalities. My father died an alcoholic at age forty-nine."

Jerry was immediately hooked. Over the next eight years he was often away from home for long periods of time. Susanne had no idea where he was. He spent all their money on drugs, and even "borrowed" from Brother Love's bank account.

In an attempt to support herself and her son, Susanne began teaching music to nine hundred students at Village Christian School, which Jarret attended from second through eighth grade. Church members gave them clothes, left food bags on their front porch, and encouraged them.

"Deep in my spirit, I had so much hope," Susanne remarks. "It was God who provided for us every step of the way."

The year 1980 was the worst. Driving to school, they would pray for Jerry. Jarret's prayer was: "Dear Jesus, please help Daddy love Mommy so she won't cry any more. Bring him home safely."

Susanne often prayed to herself, *Lord, please let Jerry be okay, and keep him from killing himself.*

"The Jerry I knew and married would come back home and be off drugs *if* he didn't die first. Mercifully, he was never arrested."

JARRET'S EYE PROBLEMS

DURING this period, Jarret's left eye was diagnosed with "lazy eye syndrome." Dr. Rosenbaum, at the UCLA Jules Stein Eye Institute, was frank about the possibility of the boy losing his sight. He needed surgery soon and perhaps more surgeries later.

There was still no guarantee his eye would work properly. Dr. Rosenbaum accepted Jarret for an experimental program that demanded daily eye exercises that required parental assistance.

One day while accompanying his son to the doctor, Jerry heard the still small voice of God tell him: "Jarret's eyes are healing. Your *spiritual* eyes are healing."

During the following months, every time Jerry slipped away to do drugs, his son's condition worsened. The doctor warned that Jarret would be taken out of the program if he didn't show progress.

Jerry realized that not being around to help with his son's eye exercises was serious. "Jarret's recovery depended on my choices. My son needed me."

On January 10, 1986, he decided to go "cold turkey" in full obedience to God. Things didn't go smoothly, however. He had strong cravings and slept more than usual.

Susanne recalls, "Jerry assured me he had stopped doing drugs, but how did I know it was true and not just an empty promise?"

Jerry cut off his entire group of drug-using friends and returned to church with his wife.

With his reformation came 20/20 vision for Jarret. The day Dr. Rosenbaum announced the astonishing results, Jarret said to his dad: "I told you. I knew the Lord would heal me."

The doctor commented, "I really do believe that your God is that powerful, because that's the only explanation for what I'm looking at."

———

Meanwhile, Susanne met with Min Whaley, a counselor at Church on the Way. Min told Susanne candidly that if she didn't fully forgive Jerry, their marriage couldn't last. Susanne would always blame him. However, if she stayed, prayed, and forgave Jerry, God would "get the victory."

Susanne chose to give her bitterness and deep hatred to God and offer her husband forgiveness.

"Jerry's parents had divorced when he was young and I knew the effect that had on him. I didn't want Jarret to experience the same thing. The Lord totally wiped my heart clean."

The dark feelings she harbored for eight years slowly dissolved.

DIVINE INTERVENTION

JERRY owed drug dealers thousands of dollars. The family was terrified that they'd come to collect. How could they be protected?

However, three years passed with no one coming. One day Jerry ran into one of his former dealers. Scared out of his mind, he wondered why Mark had never come after him.

To his surprise, the man explained: "I came up to your front door to collect the money you owed me. The gardener told me, 'Mark, you must flee. This house is protected by God.' I had no idea how he knew my name, and I didn't intend to hang around to find out!"

Jerry and Susanne were just trying to keep a roof over their heads. There was no gardener.

Another time Jerry was at a car wash. To his horror, Mongo was there. He told Mongo his testimony and how he had quit drugs. He asked him: "I've always wondered, though, why you never came after me? I owed you a lot of money."

Mongo described what had happened. "I *did* come to your front door. An elderly man was sitting on the front porch. 'Mongo,' he warned, 'You must flee. This house is protected by God.' How did he know my name?"

Then Jerry understood. The two men guarding their home were angels.

If he hadn't run into the two drug dealers, he never would have known how God was protecting his family. He remembers God's promise: "Evil can't get close to you, harm can't get through the door. He ordered His angels to guard you wherever you go (Psalm 91:10–11)."

God was also preserving Jerry and Susanne's marriage. "There is no way our marriage would have survived if one of us had Jesus in their heart and the other one didn't.

"Isn't it amazing that the very girl I broke up with because she didn't know Jesus, would hold the key to my healing and God's restoration?

"Matthew 6:33 says, 'Seek first the kingdom of God and His righteousness and all these things will be added unto you.' If you do things right and obey the Lord first and foremost, He won't hold anything back."

Susanne admits that she would "never have chosen to have a drug-addicted husband. After all, who would?"

She hadn't truly understood the distress of others before her marriage problems. Now that she's survived a nightmare, she has compassion for hurting hearts.

"The lessons we learned were life-changing. It's about the power of God. Our God is a God of restoration and healing. He is faithful to bring about the desires of our hearts. We are a perfect example of this."

BILL & NANCIE CARMICHAEL

BILL AND NANCIE CARMICHAEL were the founding publishers of Good Family Magazines, which included *Virtue, Christian Parenting Today,* and *Parents of Teenagers*, with a combined readership of over one million. These magazines are now produced by *Christianity Today*.

The Carmichaels are the owners of Deep River Books. They have written fifteen books and conduct "Habits of a Healthy Home" seminars throughout the country. Bill has served on the board of directors of the Evangelical Publisher's Association.

Their greatest delight is their expanding family—five grown children and ten grandchildren. They live in the majestic Cascade Mountains near Sisters, Oregon.

Loneliness and the feeling of being unwanted is the most terrible poverty.

Mother Teresa

Scary Times

When a dad breaks his legs and an arm, can his family survive?

BY JEANETTE CHAFFEE

BILL CARMICHAEL'S EARLY YEARS CONTAINED PAIN AND trauma. "When I was thirteen, my father, the owner of a building contracting company, fell off a scaffold and broke his legs and an arm. Even after the casts were removed, he was unable to work for another six months while he recuperated."

Yet his dad had a great sense of humor. After losing a finger in an accident, he smiled and said, "Look what I did this time."

Bill remembers times were hard for the family after these two horrible construction accidents. "We didn't have insurance, so our whole family pitched in to help. My mom worked in a store, my sister got an after-school job in a bakery, and I had a paper route. All the money went to pay the rent."

Despite the hardships, these times were some of the most enriching in his life.

"We learned lessons of faith, of letting God be the provider. I truly learned that faith wasn't just some classical biblical concept.

Trusting in the Lord became firmly embedded into me because I saw my dad's faith while growing up.

"Dad was an eternal optimist. He always quoted—and believed—'Trust in the Lord with all your heart, and lean not on your own understanding; in all your ways acknowledge Him, and He shall direct your paths (Proverbs 3:5-6).'"

When the kids were worried and one would ask, "Dad, what are we going to do?" he would consistently answer, "We're going to trust the Lord. That's what we're going to do."

Bill's mother grew up in an alcoholic home. "To escape, she married when she was sixteen and started having kids. She had me when she was twenty-one years old." It was difficult, as a young person herself, to raise children. She was always anxious.

Years later, after marrying and having five children, these lessons of faith provided Bill and Nancie with the courage to mortgage their home to start a magazine publishing company.

"Nancie and I felt God calling us to start this. It was terrifying, exciting, and exhilarating. I always keep in mind Dad quoting Proverbs 3:5-6."

The new enterprise proved to be very difficult. "In the early years we had many sleepless nights. Yet we were always able to make payroll. God always provided."

Faith has affected more than just their business. "Our family has grown—all our children are married and doing well. Through the ups and downs of family life we have been reminded of Dad Carmichael's urging us to 'trust in the Lord' no matter what!"

The Carmichaels are blessed with ten grandchildren. They continue in publishing through their company, Deep River Books.

"We are still trusting."

Not the Daughter of Their Dreams

They longed for a daughter—they got Amy

BY JEANETTE CHAFFEE

HOW WONDERFUL IT WOULD BE TO HAVE A DAUGHTER, BILL and Nancie Carmichael dreamed. After having four sons, the couple decided to adopt a girl.

The home studies were completed and the Carmichaels contacted the Bertha Holt Adoption Agency. Six months later, they received the good news they had been approved. The family had chosen a three-year-old so she'd be closer in age to their youngest.

Nancie had assumed that life with a daughter would bring great happiness to the family. "For years we fantasized how she'd wear frilly dresses, love to cook, have hobbies, read books, and 'be a lady'—someone we would be proud of."

Amy was born in Gangneung, Korea. She had been abandoned on the doorstep of a nice home. From there she was taken to the city of Chuncheon, a lovely sea resort, where she lived at the Oh Soon July Baby Home.

Years later Amy discovered her birth date—August 2, 1980—in the large record book at the city hall. Her birth mother's name, Cho Soon Ja, was also listed. It's possible that Amy's Korean name, Yung Ja (which means "Little One" in Korean), was taken from her mother.

The entire family was filled with great excitement on the day of Amy's arrival.

"How wonderful it was to see her for the first time. Our four sons—Jon, Eric, Chris, and Andy were with Bill and me when our little one arrived at SeaTac airport in Seattle."

Nancie recalls the love shown to them when "our staff had given us a shower, and we were loaded with girlie things for our new child."

The first couple of weeks were difficult, especially for Nancie. "Amy cried at night. She slept with Bill and me for the first couple of weeks, then I moved into her bedroom near ours and slept with her until she got used to her room.

"She was used to sleeping on a mat in a room with at least a dozen other small children, sharing one bathroom with 150 other kids and only having a little attention since each orphanage worker cared for twelve to fifteen children. These things leave 'permanent holes' that we didn't know of at the time."

However, as the months passed, Amy turned out to be a huge disappointment as a "dream" daughter. She was a rebellious tomboy, didn't like to read, and wasn't interested in any "girl things," such as dresses. She loved the outdoors and all that went with it.

What have we gotten ourselves into? the Carmichaels wondered.

"Why, Lord, did you give us this little girl? Don't you know that we've been waiting for a loving daughter?"

Now they ended up with an obnoxious and unaffectionate child.

They decided to pray for Amy because these problems were causing a terrible strain on their family of seven. "We prayed for our children to have strength and godly traits. As we focused our prayers on specific character traits and values, the Lord impressed upon us that we, as parents, also needed these virtues!"

Amy began discovering her own identity as a teenager. She struggled with feelings of being different—not just *ethnically*, but

The first Christmas with adopted daughter, Amy, in 1984.
(back row) Jon, Bill, Nancie, Chris. (front row) Andy, Amy, and Eric.

also due to her learning disabilities. (Her time in the orphanage had caused these due to deprivation and encephalitis.)

She learned to handle these problems with grace and tenacity. Healing came with time.

Nancie began trying to bridge the gap by spending time alone with her, "when she allowed it."

Once, when the two of them went to the movies, Amy asked, "Will I ever belong anywhere?" Her mother replied, "I know how you feel."

Nancie reminded her about always walking close to Jesus— and resembling Him. Then they gave each other a bear hug, held hands, got the giggles, and had a great time at the show.

She understood the importance of allowing her daughter the freedom to express her pain. "Just to listen to your child say how they feel is healing. It's so healing to be understood. Don't discount the pain. As a mom, I wanted to fix it, but I couldn't."

Despite the disappointments of receiving a "gift" that was so different from their dreams, the couple gradually learned to understand the Father's heart.

"We began to see her differently and appreciate her. Her compassion for people. Her longing to give money to any beggar we passed. Her understanding of what it's like to be homeless and unloved. Her talents. That it was okay for her to want to wear jeans and be a tomboy. That she didn't need to fit into the mold of being an 'ideal' daughter."

Nancie thought: *How could God stand to be around sinners? How could Jesus be so patient with rebellious people?*

The Bible verse that became meaningful to them was, "He is the high priest and truly sympathizes with our weaknesses and understands our temptations (Hebrews 4:15)."

Yes, Amy has many learning disabilities, but the family appreciates her dauntless persistence. She is a reminder to them of how faithful God is with people.

The couple is encouraged during chaotic moments with Philippians 1:6: "He who began a good work in you will carry it on to completion until the day of Christ Jesus."

Everyone has learned what unconditional love looks like. Nancie agrees that "our whole family—especially me—had big-time lessons to learn about love and acceptance."

Amy is now married and working in a restaurant, helping to support her husband as he attends college.

"We can't imagine life without her now because she's such a love to us."

No, not the daughter of their dreams. Far better.

Bill and Nancie with their grandkids at summer camp in Oregon.

SANDRA ALDRICH

SANDRA P. ALDRICH is president and CEO of Bold Words, Inc. A popular inspirational speaker, she has authored or coauthored twenty books and served as senior editor of *Focus on the Family* magazine. Sandra has been a guest on *The 700 Club*, *Prime Time American*, and *Focus on the Family*. She earned her master's degree from Eastern Michigan University. She has two married children and lives in the shadow of Pikes Peak in scenic Colorado.

Rainbows come after rain…
like us too, happiness
comes after sorrow.

Delfin

Unprepared

Getting married, she never imagines death

BY JEANETTE CHAFFEE

FEBRUARY FIFTH MARKS THE DAY WHEN SANDRA ALDRICH stepped into marriage and a life of unlimited potential. "Don and I were filled with youthful energy and bright dreams," Sandra recalls.

"We had deep faith, college degrees, and a solid work ethic. A wonderful future was ours, and we marched toward our concept of the Perfect Family—complete with two beautiful children, the colonial house, two cars, and a summer place.

"We hadn't planned on brain cancer."

Suddenly she was widowed with two children to raise: Jay (ten) and Holly (eight). *God, you took the wrong parent,* Sandra thought. *Don was fun, godly, and had laughter that rolled around the walls.*

What should she do now?

The days following the funeral left her despondent and wanting to withdraw. "But I had two young children who needed me. They had lost their dad physically; I didn't want them to lose me emotionally. I didn't want to be one of those hand-wringing widows who insists her grief is greater than what anyone else has experienced. I believe my grief is something I will never get *over* but rather *through."*

She had never imagined having to face the loss of a husband.

Life had been peaceful growing up in Southeastern Kentucky — deep within the beautiful Appalachian Mountains. She lived in a microscopic town named Keith. She describes it as having a sliver of a highway with homes jammed up against the mountainside. It was easy to find the church: the only other building was Miz Bailey's general store.

"I wanted to be a wife and mother, have a big garden, and learn to quilt. That background never prepared me to 'sign on' for widowhood. I had everything figured out."

During those first years, she clung to Isaiah 54:5. "Your Creator will be your husband. The Lord Almighty is His name."

At night Sandra prayed for comfort and peace. "Jesus, you have promised to be my husband. Good husbands should _____." She would fill in the blank with "give me guidance" or "adore me" — whatever reassurance she needed. Then she'd get a good night's sleep, believing that He'd give her direction.

Although Don's death was unfair, Sandra never blamed God. *I don't want to bite the hand that feeds me.* She prayed to a real Being who actively listened to her concerns, not empty air.

Working hard to be available to her children and listening to their pain were of key importance to her.

"During these times, as well as during Don's long illness before his death, often the verse 'Be still and know that I am God (Psalm 46:10)' would pop into my head." Having Scripture memorized allowed the Lord to comfort her.

One day, much to her bewilderment, God's whisperings stopped. "I no longer heard God. No remembrances of the Word. No warm feelings. No love."

What changed? Didn't He care? Where *was* He?

Then she remembered the time when Jay was little and had a terrible case of chickenpox. The rash was all over, even on the soles of his feet. She had held him on her lap for hours. She didn't talk, tell stories, or play games with him. She just held him.

Suddenly she got it. That was what God was doing with her!

He still cared, though she didn't always feel His presence. God never stopped holding and loving her.

She is still unprepared for the future. But secure on God's lap, she's ready for anything.

"I concentrate on what I have left instead of what I have lost."

Sandra in 2013.

I Choose Joy

A unique way to cope with breast cancer

BY JEANETTE CHAFFEE

WHIRLWINDS OF ACTIVITY. LITTLE SLEEP. INCESSANT whining. Changing diapers. That was Sandra Aldrich's life as a young mother.

"There was always one kid I couldn't find. I was always chasing one or the other."

Exhaustion came with the territory. She told herself, "I'll get a decent night's sleep when I get to heaven!"

Looking back, she should have enjoyed motherhood more. "I wish I had slowed down and hadn't tried to impress the in-laws so much. I was always hurrying, even if we were just going for a walk! Isn't that ridiculous?"

She learned how important it is to grab moments. "A friend of mine and her kids used popsicle sticks on their lawn to create a tiny fenced-in area. Every day they would check it out. *What did they see? What was in the grass?* It opened their eyes to a whole new world. We should all get down and check the bugs out. Study the ants."

Children need fun and balance in life. When Sandra lived in snowy Michigan, she kept large plastic garbage bags in her car's trunk. She'd stop on the way to her parents' house so her kids could use the bags for sledding down hills.

Soon after her husband, Don, died at the age of thirty-nine, Sandra resolved to choose joy in spite of hardships and sorrow. "In the midst of grief, we can wring our hands and say, 'Life is so hard.' Or we can laugh and say, 'Isn't life great that I've been blessed in this way and the Lord is with me?'

"I can lament the lost experiences or I can rejoice in the Lord's presence and how He helped us build a new life as a family of three."

Sandra was able to use these insights to bring comfort to others. While serving as the senior editor of *Focus on the Family* magazine, she had a telephone conversation with a young mother.

"The woman told me she wasn't dying from breast cancer. She was *living* with it. What a great attitude — and example."

In the middle of their serious talk about death, the caller's preschooler came in clutching several kittens. "I heard her ask him, 'What are you doing?' The boy responded, 'I want to put them in the freezer so they can cool off because it's a very hot day.'"

Both women burst into outrageous laughter.

"That's just the way life is: tragedy, loss, death, and laughter all rolled together. Though this young mother was facing health challenges, she chose joy."

ANNE GRAHAM LOTZ

ANNE (GRAHAM) LOTZ is the second of five children born to evangelist Billy and Ruth Graham. Anne founded one of the first classes of Bible Study Fellowship on the east coast and taught BSF to over five hundred women in North Carolina for twelve years. She spoke at the International Congress of Itinerant Evangelists in Amsterdam twice, the only woman to be a plenary speaker.

She founded her own nonprofit organization and is on the board of the Billy Graham Evangelistic Association. The *New York Times* named her one of the five most influential evangelists in the United States. Anne has been awarded six honorary doctorate degrees. She is the author of more than a dozen books, and she has spoken all over the world.

Anne and her husband, Danny, have three grown children and three grandchildren.

*I long to hear You say to me
one day, "Well done, good
and faithful servant."*

Max Lucado

A Sense of Loss ...
a Sense of Gain

A loving daughter and father are forced apart

BY JEANETTE CHAFFEE

DESPITE BEING A WORLD-FAMOUS AUTHOR, BIBLE TEACHER, and evangelist, Anne Graham Lotz had challenges. The second oldest child of Billy and Ruth Graham admits, "I grew up with failures, struggles, and many inadequacies."

When she was seven, she accepted the Jesus her father preached about and whom her family worshiped. "Jesus forgave my sins and became my own personal Savior."

Anne received public, private, and homeschooled education—even skipping a grade. "When I went to public high school, the response of my classmates and the community was different than many people would imagine."

Her peers never asked about her famous father. "They were our neighbors. We bumped into them at the grocery store. People weren't impressed with Daddy or his reputation as a preacher."

But Anne was overly worried about *her* image. "At one point a friend told me, 'You're a phony.'"

Was this true? What kind of person was I?

Finally, Anne admitted: "My friend was right. I needed to stop caring so much about other people's opinions. I thought I had to live up to a reputation. I couldn't please everyone in the world anyway. I needed to live my life to please God. He knew I could take the responsibility and overcome my worry about my image and other people's opinions."

NOT ENOUGH TIME WITH FAMILY

"ONE of the most difficult things I have faced has been that my family of seven hasn't had much time together."

With her father's incredibly busy schedule and travels, no matter how hard the family tried to find time together, there were extended periods when they were apart.

She likens this sense of loss to those who are widowed or divorced. She quotes Psalm 27:9–10, which says: "Don't leave me now. Don't forsake me, O God of my salvation. For if my father and mother should abandon me, You would welcome and comfort me."

Her parents never forsook her, yet, in a sense, it applies. "The verse is a special promise. God makes the loss up in Himself."

What helped was that her family shares the same worldview for reaching people. "We love to serve, worship, work, and honor our Lord. I believe that my family has cohesiveness and deep love for each other in spite of not spending a lot of time together."

In addition to the family being apart, there have been attacks against them. Anne points to her husband's dental clinic being burned to the ground, her parents' serious illnesses, and her son's battle with cancer.

Yet she loves being a member of the Graham family. "They are wonderful. I'd want to know them even if we weren't relatives.

We're strong-willed personalities and all very different—yet we are all friends! My siblings and parents are stimulating."

Anne recognizes that God chose where she would be born. "It was His grace that put me in Billy Graham's family. That's not something I did or anything I deserved. He just plopped me here."

She can't imagine having a different mother, father, or other siblings. "I *love* them. I praise God I was placed here."

According to Anne, she is most thankful for one thing about her home life: there's no glitz in the family. It's a family that wants to serve—a Christ-centered home. "I was born and raised to know the Lord, love the Lord, and be motivated to serve the Lord. It is

Billy Graham reading to his girls in 1955, at their home in North Carolina. (left to right) Ruth, Anne (kneeling), and Gigi.

my parents' legacy." The example was set in her home. "When we worship, we must serve Him. We can't just sit and do nothing.

"I'm here to testify that life in Christ is much sweeter than anything on an earthly level."

A GLOBAL FOCUS

ANNE considers it a privilege to use her gifts — such as her speaking ability — not for herself, but for God's kingdom. Ministering both in the U.S. and abroad, she has learned firsthand the importance of global awareness. "It's far more than just our community. We must open our eyes to a much broader world."

Anne emphasizes this with her two daughters and son. She believes it is important for children not to become so self-centered they forget there's a world that needs Jesus. She shares reports of her overseas ministry with her family and is delighted that they know what the Lord is doing.

She took her children on mission trips to Amsterdam and Moscow. Her daughters have visited Spain and France; the youngest also traveled to South Africa.

"Their eyes are open. I want them to know that America is not the center of the universe." She has no idea where God will lead. "I don't know if the Lord will call them into ministry or not, but I want them to have the exposure — the planet's larger than our own immediate circle."

For years, her son Jonathan corresponded with an itinerant pastor in South Africa. She believes Brother Harry has had as large an impact on Jonathan's life as anyone in their family.

ROLE MODELS

ANNE'S life is different because of stellar examples: her mother, her grandmother, her mentor Miss Johnson, and, of course, her father.

Ruth Graham was born and raised in China. This experience gave her a wonderful perspective which helped her manage the tensions and pressures of life in the Graham home.

"She had such a love for Christ and the Bible," Anne tells. "It showed even in the way she handled its pages."

Yet her mother had a playful sense of humor. Once when Ruth and her husband were dining at the White House, President Johnson asked Billy Graham, "Who should I pick for a running mate?"

Ruth gently kicked her husband. Rubbing his shin in mock pain, Billy asked, "Why did you kick me under the table?"

"You can give opinions on spiritual matters, but you're to stay out of politics."

"You're exactly right," he said, and changed the subject.

When dinner was over, Ruth and Lady Bird Johnson exited the dining room first. President Johnson took advantage of the opportunity to turn to his guest and say, "Well, now that your wife is gone, tell me what you really think."

Anne doesn't know how the conversation continued after that, but her family always gets a laugh out of the story.

Another woman who greatly influenced Anne is her grandmother. "I treasured her love and her acceptance of me. She taught me how to read the Bible."

Her grandparents experienced a difficult life as missionaries in the 1920s. "Grandpa Bell took his wife to China when she was a bride of six weeks. She worked at the women's clinic where he was the surgeon.

"Grandma bore children in China and buried one." Just *living* was challenging — before they could drink the water, it had to pass through five layers of cheesecloth.

"It's amazing what Grandma put up with. She had migraine headaches, yet she was such a woman of God. She was very loving. I absolutely adored her."

———————

A third person who had a profound impact on Anne's ministry is the founder of Bible Study Fellowship (BSF), Miss Audrey Johnson, a brilliant, well-educated woman who mentored Anne.

"Miss Johnson trained me during the last five years before she retired. She had the *most* wonderful love for Christ. It was her love for Christ and the way she taught the Word that had real power."

Anne assisted in establishing BSF on the east coast. Over four thousand attended her weekly studies in her home town of Raleigh, North Carolina. "Bible Study Fellowship has affected our community on every level."

———————

Of course, Billy Graham is a major role model in Anne's life. As a father, he was "kind, yet firm. He had a certain look. None of us kids wanted that look! I'd get frightened and straighten up quickly."

But Anne's dad lived the way he taught. "He's just the same at home as behind the pulpit. There's no difference. He's gracious, warm, and affectionate. As Daddy gets older, he gets even sweeter. I love being around him."

Even at his advanced age, Billy still always watches the evening news on TV and keeps up on current affairs. He subscribes to many of the leading newspapers in the world. "At least he'll read the headlines."

Because of her father's habits, Anne and her siblings grew up with an awareness of the world. Having visitors in their home also contributed. Another factor was that "Daddy would come home and give us reports."

Anne was also inspired by her father's love for the Word. "I sensed his tremendous respect for the presence of Christ in his life as well as his calling. It kept him from falling into the traps that some other people do. He's more aware of his accountability to Christ than to anything else."

Even the secular world respects him.

"You know, Daddy was said to be the first or second most influential person in the United States in the twentieth century." According to Gallup's top ten list of Most Admired Men, February 2014 marked the fifty-seventh time that her father made the list since 1955 — more than anyone else.

"It shows the wisdom of the people who chose and voted for him." To her amazement, they were "picking someone who is strongly identified with the gospel of Jesus Christ. This is honoring for a man who has honored God all his life.

"I'm grateful for Daddy's ministry. God has given him such a broad platform to share the gospel."

NEVER-ENDING MINISTRY

ANNE has met people all over the world who learned of Jesus through her father's preaching. More people are hearing the gospel as a result of his ministry than ever before.

"It's a humbling thing. It's an enormous responsibility to make sure that when my father's voice is silenced, for whatever reason, other voices will carry the message of the gospel to new generations.

"I heard Daddy say he wants to be remembered for being faithful to Christ. His legacy will be: faithful in service right up until the end."

EDITH SCHAEFFER

EDITH SCHAEFFER and her husband, Francis, founded L'Abri Fellowship in Huemoz, Switzerland. L'Abri—which means "The Shelter" in French—began in 1955 and it continues to be a world-famous community.

Study centers have grown to include additional locations in the United States, Canada, Sweden, the United Kingdom, Holland, Germany, and Brazil. People seeking intellectual honesty come to ask questions about God, the relevance of faith and culture, and the biblical meaning of life.

Edith wrote seventeen books, all of which are still influential. In 1979 she was given a Gold Medallion Award from the Evangelical Christian Publishers Association for *Affliction*. Mrs. Schaeffer is listed in Helen Hosier's *100 Christian Women Who Changed the Twentieth Century*.

She enjoyed interacting with L'Abri students and stayed involved with the organization until her death. Mrs. Schaeffer had four children, fifteen grandchildren, and sixteen great-grandchildren, and loved spoiling all of them. She lived in Switzerland until she died at the age of ninety-eight on March 30, 2013.

She did not see age as a reminder to slow down...

Edith Rachel Merritt Seville Schaeffer was born in Wenchow, China. She lived her last years in a lovely 1683 chalet in Gryon, Switzerland... surrounded with the beloved witnesses of her life: precious antiques, her favorite gift of a Steinway baby grand piano, dozens of paintings by her son Franky, and linen drapes.... Every day Edith dressed and applied perfume. She died wearing a new Ralph Lauren nightgown from Macy's in New York, in clean sheets and in her own bed—as she had wished all her life. It was the night between Holy Friday and Holy Saturday.

Edith marked her life with the expression of rich ideas.... She lived her life as a work of art, an exhibition of true significance and a portrait of a generous, stunning, and creative personality. With much imagination, she served her meals with decorations made from twigs, moss, field flowers, and stones.

Duncan Kabiru, from Kenya, once remarked, "This is the first place where I see the beauty of the truth of the Bible consistently carried over into all areas of life."

Edith was in all things generous. She used all the royalties she received from her books to provide family reunions every year.

While Edith was visiting the island of Elba, saxophonist Sonny Rollins noticed her beauty and rhythm as she danced to his music. He came off the stage and danced with her.

From the death announcement by The Schaeffer Foundation
(theschaefferfoundation.com)

Our deepest instinct is heaven.
Heaven is the ache in our
bones, the splinter in our heart.
Like the whisper of faraway
waves we hear crashing in
the whorls of a conch shell,
the music of heaven echoes,
faint, elusive, haunting…
The instinct for heaven is
just that: homesickness.
All your longings — for the
place you grew up, for the
taste of raspberry tarts that
your mother once pulled
hot from the oven, for that
bend in the river where your
father took you fishing as a
child… These are the things
seen that conjure in our
emotions the things unseen.
The writer of Ecclesiastes
[in 3:11] said: "…they cannot
fathom what God has done
from beginning to end."

Mark Buchanan

Reflections of Death and Heaven

A dying man's last words to his sweetheart

BY JEANETTE CHAFFEE

EDITH'S HUSBAND, DR. FRANCIS SCHAEFFER, A WRITER AND highly-esteemed Christian evangelical speaker, died on May 15, 1984. It was just ten days after moving into a new home in Minnesota.

"He had me buy a house in Rochester and have the furniture brought from Switzerland, because he wanted to come home once more," Edith said.

That day he was in and out of consciousness. At 4 a.m. he whispered to her, "Keep on from strength to strength." She knew this was from Psalm 84:7, even though he couldn't say anything more. At that moment, he stopped breathing.

Despite her husband's death, Edith understood that she was to continue the work of L'Abri, their foundation for studying biblical truth. "When Francis told me that verse, I felt strongly that I was to keep on and not stop."

She was assured that her husband was with the Lord in heaven. "At the moment of his death, it seemed that in my imagination, I saw him going out through the glass doors between the trees and on up into the sky."

Reaching for the Bible, she thought: *The fact that Francis is absent is very clear. It's only in this Book that I can depend upon the fact that the apostle Paul said, "absent from the body, present with the Lord (2 Corinthians 5:8)" is true.*

"I couldn't see his presence there. But I knew from that definite declaration that yes, that's where he had gone. I hadn't seen his arrival, but I knew he was there."

Edith was comforted that in the few days before her husband's death, their four children were all able to visit with him. The Sunday before he died, Dr. Schaeffer propped himself up in bed and listened to the *Coral Ridge Hour,* with Dr. D. James Kennedy. "Am I never going to speak to the evangelical world again?" he softly asked his family.

Susan, their daughter, reassured him: "Dad, you're going to go on speaking through your books."

His influence continues to have a world impact. Edith once recalled: "What Susan said to Francis that day is true. His books, such as *Genesis in Space and Time* and *The God Who is There*, are being read now more than ever. And it's very, very special."

"Where do you want to be buried?" Franky had asked his father one day. "In Philadelphia, next to your father? Or in Switzerland, next to your mother? Or do you want to be buried here?"

Francis turned to his wife. "Edith, where do *you* want to live?"

She told him, "I will live here because I have purchased the home and brought all the furniture over from Switzerland at your request."

That settled it. "Then I want to be buried here."

So Franky assisted his mother in purchasing a cemetery plot in Rochester. Edith often placed flowers on his tombstone. She planted twelve geraniums there the year he had been gone twelve years. To Edith, taking care of the gravesite was like caring for your garden or home's front walkway.

"Make it as pleasant as possible. Not just for those you love, but also for strangers. Bring the pleasure of your creativity to other people."

Edith didn't believe in continually living in grief. "I don't like setting life aside. Life goes on. Of course, I miss him."

She found comfort in heaven and what Christ has planned for His children. "I am reminded of 1 Corinthians 2:9, which says, 'Eye has not seen, ear has not heard, neither has entered into the heart of man the things which God has prepared for those who love Him.'

"I have no idea what heaven will be like. The beauty! No one can ever imagine how beautiful it will be.

"When I think of heaven, I think of the Architect of this world. Just look at the beauty here on earth: the Swiss Alps at sunset, the wonder of a rose, and water droplets turning into diamonds by the sun. Snow falling on a treetop, a house roof, or a mountain slope. The wonder of waves crashing against the rocks. Listen to the music! All this is nothing compared to heaven."

Planned by Accident

An inquisitive visitor begins a trend

BY JEANETTE CHAFFEE

EDITH SCHAEFFER HAD WONDERFUL MEMORIES OF HER missionary childhood in China. "I've always enjoyed people. Everyone at our compound was fun. I was fond of my playmates, all busily talking away."

It was a happy time in her life. Edith left China to attend Beaver College in Pennsylvania. There she met and fell in love with Francis Schaeffer. They married in 1935 and over the next decade had three daughters. While Dr. Schaeffer attended seminary, Edith worked to support them as a tailor of fine wedding dresses and men's suits.

In 1947, God led the couple into missions to work with young people in Europe. They moved to Huemoz, Switzerland, and Edith gave birth to a son in 1952.

Just as their lives were becoming settled, a twist came from an unexpected source. Edith received a call from their daughter, Susan, who was away at college. "May I bring a girlfriend home for the weekend?"

Edith readily consented. During the visit, the girl asked Susan's dad many provocative questions about God. She left thinking, *I've got to go back to their home again because I can't believe the answers Dr. Schaeffer gives.*

That started a steady stream of visitors and was the beginning of L'Abri, a place for conversation about God. Nothing was planned; it just happened.

"Susan was the one bringing people home," Edith admitted. "Without us imagining anything, she actually started L'Abri."

The L'Abri community gradually grew. Today, residential study centers exist on three continents (North America, Europe, and South America). People come from around the world and are welcome to ask intellectual questions about God, the Bible, and how Christianity impacts daily life and culture.

With constant visitors, Edith got to display her creativity and love of beauty as a hostess. Some people call this "hospitality." Edith carefully explained that it's much more than that.

"My mind keeps racing. I plan and execute events. For example, if I'm receiving thirty-six young Chinese pianists, I prepare the refreshments and our home. Candles. I must have candles! I'll have thirty-six of them."

Preparing for such events and paying attention to the details—musing over the choice of flowers, the food, and the table settings—brought her joy. Edith's goal was for everyone to have a meaningful time. She meticulously planned the menu and sketched out seating arrangements. She wanted to "give people pleasure and connect those who will enjoy each other."

Edith exemplified a servant's heart; nothing was too mundane for her. "I always did the cooking and sewing. My attitude was basically to free Francis so he could answer questions. He would sit at the head of the dining room table or by the fireplace."

Jeanette Chaffee

October 30
1996

Dear Jeanette,
It was good talking
to you, and I am
glad you have
used ideas in
this book so well
with love
and prayer
for your future,
in the Lamb

Edith Schaeffer

In an extraordinary personal gesture, Edith elaborately autographed her book, *Hidden Art*, for Jeanette.

Whatever she was serving—homemade soup, a snack of cheese and crackers, or an elegant dinner—always brought joy to everyone.

Edith remembered the unusual hours when great conversations took place. "It might be 2 a.m. and I would bring hot chocolate or food to revive everyone. I would return to the kitchen and do the dishes."

She compared her role and activities to "making the backdrop so the play can go on." She wanted folks to feel free to discuss matters without interruption.

Often there were more than fifty people at their home for a meal. Sometimes this was overwhelming. "I was all alone washing and drying the dishes. At that time we didn't have a dishwasher."

One night she'd just had it. "I was careful to put all the dishes on a tray. I whirled around and *whoosh!* Everything flew onto the floor."

She broke into tears. A man in charge of the broadcasting equipment at the house—there to record her husband's talk that evening—rushed in to see what caused all the noise.

"I'm sorry," Edith explained. "I just got mad because I'm here washing dishes alone. I lost my cool."

The man quietly helped her pick everything up and said he was sorry.

Telling the story years later, Edith laughed and said, "That ended in a nice manner."

It was like so much in her life that hadn't been planned—a willing attitude made all the difference.

PHYLISS MASTERS

Philip and **PHYLISS MASTERS** served together as missionaries in Dutch New Guinea (now Papua, Indonesia) from 1961 until Phil's murder by cannibals on September 25, 1968. She was three months pregnant at the time. Relying on God's strength, she and their five children continued living in the area until her return to the United States in 1987. Phyliss trained locals to teach the Bible in their own villages. Later, she conducted seminars at mission locations in the Swart Valley (now called Toli).

Today Phyliss speaks at churches and conferences and is on the missions committee at LeMars Bible Church in Iowa. She loves using her gift of hospitality and she delights in her thirteen grandchildren and a great-granddaughter.

It didn't happen overnight.
Not as expected.
Not as chosen.

But it happened.

Marc Zeedar and Jeanette Chaffee

162

Murdered by Lords of the Earth

Turning tragedy into triumph

BY JEANETTE CHAFFEE

HOW DID GOD BRING TOGETHER AN IOWA FARMER, AN Aussie, a witch doctor's son, a tribe of cannibals, brutal murders, an orphaned child, and a crashed airplane to teach "lords of the earth" about the true Lord of the Earth?

REACHING THE YALI

IN the 1960s, deep in the mountains of Dutch New Guinea (also called Irian Jaya), lived an obscure tribe of violent headhunters who believed themselves to be the "lords of the earth." They were known as the Yali and they had never heard the gospel.

Yet God decided they needed to hear His message.

GROWING UP IN IOWA

Philip Masters grew up on a farm near Mapleton, Iowa. He loved farming, accepted the Lord Jesus as his personal Savior, and decided to become an agricultural missionary. While attending Westmar College, he went to district youth meetings where he met Phyliss Wills, who had recently become a Christian.

Phil had grown up only eighty miles from her, but they had never met. They began dating during her senior year in high school. Phyliss continued her education at the University of South Dakota. They married on February 1, 1953, and Phil graduated from Cornell College that same year.

In 1955, they left Iowa to attend Prairie Bible Institute in Alberta, Canada. Baby Crissie was born that year. Curtis came the following year, and Becky arrived in 1959.

While studying in Alberta, they felt God's leading to go to Dutch New Guinea. "It was a hard struggle for me to give in to the Lord and submit to

The Masters family in the 1960s: Phyliss, Phil, and their young children.

His direction," Phyliss admits. "My life was ordinary. I was overly conscious of my many inadequacies and lack of outstanding gifts."

She asked God to change her heart and He did.

They did not have an unusual burden or emotional feeling for these Stone Age people. Since they knew this was what the Lord wanted them to do, they simply put one foot in front of the other in obedience to Him. The Lord reminded Phyliss in John 15:14 that "You are my friends if you do whatsoever I command you."

The couple's special verse in those years was "Faithful is He who calls you, and He also will bring it to pass (1 Thessalonians 5:24)."

That was a powerful reminder to Phil and Phyliss that unless "the Lord builds the house they labor in vain (Psalm 127:1)" and it is "not by might nor by power, but by My Spirit (Zechariah 4:6)."

ARRIVING IN DUTCH NEW GUINEA

In 1961, Phil and Phyliss boarded a freighter headed for Australia, and then flew to Dutch New Guinea to work with the Dani people. Settling in the Swart Valley at Karubaga, they received a warm reception. Their daughter Crissie describes how they were "surrounded by throngs of curious Dani covered with grease and soot."

Some of these men and women would become lifelong friends of the missionaries. Many would become brothers and sisters

Phil Masters with colleague David Martin, at the first baptism in Karubaga in 1963.

in Christ. Phyliss remembers witnessing the first baptisms and communions, and how some of the Dani burned their fetishes.

(Fetishes were charms the natives thought had magical powers or were inhabited by spirits, so destroying them was turning their back on their traditional superstitious beliefs.)

While living in Karubaga, Phyliss helped establish literacy classes. She and Phil learned the Dani language, taught the Word of God, and assisted in day-to-day matters such as the upkeep of the grounds. She also homeschooled her two eldest children.

Crissie, Curt, and Becky had fun with their new playmates. They introduced Dani children to the large swing set their dad had built. It was a big hit with the kids!

MEETING STAN AND PAT DALE

A missionary couple from Australia, Stan and Pat Dale, also lived in the area. A friendship soon developed between all of them, even though their backgrounds were so different.

The Dales: Pat, Stan, and daughters, Joy and Janet.

Phil and Phyliss had stable homes. Stan's life had been everything to the contrary. Raised in an atmosphere of poverty and drunkenness, he helped in the family bakery until his parents filed for bankruptcy.

His dad, a staunch atheist, refused to expose his children to anything about God. However, as a teenager, while visiting the library, Stan began reading Christian books. He attended a meeting where he heard that Jesus loved him and died on the cross to forgive his sins. Stan accepted the Lord as his Savior that night. It was November 14, 1933.

When World War II started, he joined the Australian infantry, and served as a commando in the jungles of Papua New Guinea. To his surprise, he found churches and discovered that some natives were Christians.

The amazing sight of the distant mountain ranges captured Stan's attention. He wondered about the people living there and how they would ever hear the truth about Jesus Christ. He thought, *I want to come back here and bring the gospel to those remote people.*

He sensed God calling him to "go beyond the ranges."

Stan didn't know that thousands of cannibals filled the Pass Valley and lived in the eastern highlands.

In 1944, he finished his military service and returned to Australia. He began training at Sydney Missionary and Bible

Stan Dale working on translating the Bible with a local.

College. Shortly after graduation, Stan met a young woman, Patricia McCormack, who was training to be a nurse.

They married November 5, 1949 and moved to Dutch New Guinea where they began serving as missionaries. Over the years they had five children (Wesley, Rodney, Hilary, Joy, and Janet).

On March 20, 1961, the couple were commissioned to go to a remote, unnamed valley (later known as Heluk) near the Yali, a tribe of cannibals. They were to partner in the work with Bruno de Leeuw. Pat and the kids stayed behind while the men went ahead to Ninia to build an airstrip.

Construction conditions were extremely difficult. Eight Christian Dani tribesmen helped. Slowly, over the next ten and a half months, they carved a suitable airstrip out of the mountainside, one shovelful of rock and dirt at a time. They used no power tools.

The Yali were warriors who proudly proclaimed themselves "lords of the earth." (They were only "lords" of the island they thought was the entire world.)

Stan Dale and Bruno de Leeuw in the Heluk Valley.

Their culture was infused with trust in powerful ghosts, spirit worship, and the magic of *ap hwalon* (witch doctors). They considered outsiders *duong,* spirits in the shape of men. Yali believed in *kembu* – powerful spirits – and their lives revolved around them.

War cries and battles were almost daily events; the Yali fought with arrows and bamboo spears.

Dongla, the witch doctor's son, greeting one of the first missionaries to New Guinea, Bruno de Leeuw, in 2011.

However, not all Yali were vicious. Dongla, son of a witch doctor, welcomed Stan from the beginning. Dongla had his doubts about the spirit world, but he dared not share his concerns because the penalty for breaking sacred taboos meant death—either by man or by an evil spirit. He had seen many die in brutal ways.

He confided with Stan about his uncertainty.

"Even before the coming of the white man, I had begun to doubt the 'traditions of the ancestor.' In my heart of hearts, I even questioned the validity of the sacred lore passed on to me by my witch doctor father, Andeng."

Dongla decided to trust in God, against his father's desires. "Either I believe what the white man is teaching and put my confidence in the goodness of the Creator God to protect me or I continue to live a lie."

The gospel gave Dongla hope, in contrast to the Yali religion, and eventually he took a strong stand for Jesus Christ. "As for me, I will trust myself to God."

A small group of Yali believers joined with him in this newfound faith in the Lord. Missionary John Wilson recalls, "The trickle of interest gradually grew."

In early 1962, Phil Masters arrived in Ninia to assist Stan and Bruno. Stan greatly appreciated Phil's willingness to help. The airstrip was critical because airplanes were the easiest and sometimes the only source of transportation into the jungles, mountains, and swamplands.

During his visit, Phil watched Stan teach a tiny group of Yali believers. The Lord began to burden Phil's heart for them.

The first successful landing of an aircraft on the completed airstrip occurred on March 22nd. The men were jubilant. Stan told Pat that she and the children could now join him in Ninia. They lived in a hut for three months before moving into a house in June, where Pat homeschooled her children and taught Bible stories to the Yali women.

MOVING TO KORUPUN

In 1963, Phil and Phyliss moved to Korupun among the Kimyal people. They began learning that language and gaining the people's trust. Phyliss was also caring for her newborn, Rob.

The couple shared Bible stories and began literacy work. Daily life consisted of building a house, growing vegetables and fruit trees, and buying firewood. They also raised chickens, fish, and rabbits.

Their farming activities helped improve the lives of the Kimyal. As they began trusting the Americans, the couple provided them with medical care.

It was a beginning. They had never heard of a loving Lord who was *all* powerful and who could give them "abundant life." A few young men prayed the prayer of salvation, but progress was gradual. Phyliss feels it was a privilege to have had a small part in bringing the gospel to the tribe.

Today, the Kimyal say that the Masters were the first to bring them the Word of God.

Yali warrior, with arrows, in 1974.

DANGEROUS HOSTILITY AND YALI MARTYRS

In 1965, the Dale family went back to Australia on furlough for one year. Another missionary, Costas Macris and his family, took their place in Ninia. During this time, Dongla's father, Andeng, became seriously ill. As the most powerful witch doctor, he was greatly respected. Costas prayed for him and Andeng recovered.

However, Andeng refused to believe that the white man's God healed him. He continued to encourage the belief in fetishes and use of them escalated.

When the Dales returned, Stan decided to confront the growing problem. "The danger will remain as long as the power of the fetish men is unchallenged. If their power is broken, immediately this whole area will be wide open to the gospel."

He challenged the Yali Christians to renounce their fetishes, and some, including Dongla, burned them. This increased the hostility between fetish users, Yali Christians, and missionaries. While visiting a Yali village, Stan was shot with five barbed arrows. People didn't survive from wounds that serious. But he fully recovered. The Yali were amazed.

Yali man with headnet and pig tusks (a sign of wealth).

During all this, Stan continued emphasizing the importance of sharing the Good News. He challenged the Yali Christians: "Who among you will go preach the gospel?"

Yekwara and Bengwok volunteered. They set off for the lower Heluk Valley. A group of angry Yali chased and shot them with arrows. Yekwara and Bengwok became the first Yali martyrs.

It was a terrible blow to both the missionaries and the Yali believers.

AMBUSHED

In 1968, Stan wanted Phil to join him on a trek through the Solo and Seng Valleys to make contact with a tribe of unknown Yali. Phil agreed.

Stan Dale on a trek.

On September 17, Stan and Pat completed preparations for the trip. Stan gathered all the gear, including a nylon tent, map and compass, rope, matches, can opener, medical kit, and a New Testament. Their food consisted of rice, corned beef, powdered milk, and tea.

The next morning the Mission Aviation Fellowship (MAF) plane arrived at Ninia to pick up the Dales. It was a short flight to Korupun, where the Masters lived. Phyliss welcomed them with her famous cinnamon buns. The family would stay at the Masters' home while the men were on their mission.

This was back before cell phones, so the only communication with the men during their venture would be via handheld radio. The wives would be in charge of the main radio at home base. Phil promised to contact Phyliss every day at 5 p.m.

Early Thursday the company set out. Four Dani carriers helped transport the heavy packs. Almost immediately they were caught in a downpour. The rains continued throughout the night and washed away local bridges.

That evening, in spite of the miserable weather, Phil spoke in a cheery voice, telling his wife they had reached the first village safely. Though Phyliss was delighted to hear from him, she was dismayed to discover that her radio wasn't working properly. She could receive transmissions, but couldn't send out—so asking questions was impossible.

The torrential rains continued, and Friday evening Phyliss became concerned when Phil didn't call. There was again no communication on Saturday. Phyliss didn't know if her radio was completely broken or if the men couldn't contact her because of the terrible weather. What could she do? A new radio couldn't be flown in until the storm ended.

To the incredible relief of the wives, Phil radioed in on Sunday, and everything was fine with the men. Unfortunately, communication was still one-way.

Then on Monday, there was no call.

The next night, Phyliss still couldn't transmit, but she did hear from the men. The report from the field was positive. Phil said that their campsite was almost ready. Stan was excited that they were about to meet the Yali.

It was the last time Phyliss would hear her husband's voice.

As Stan, Phil, and their four Dani carriers crossed the fields of sweet potatoes, hidden Yali watched them. They wanted to kill the invaders immediately, but they knew that shedding blood near their crops would incur the wrath of the *kembu*, and the harvest would fail.

So they stalked the men. They watched them camp for the night by the Seng river and waited for them to head up the narrow trail in the morning. Then they attacked, shooting over one hundred arrows at close range, killing both missionaries and two of the Dani tribesmen.

The two remaining Dani dropped their packs in terror and took off running. They didn't stop for twenty-five hours, climbing the steep mountain range to the north.

Yali man carrying a rain cape in a net bag and wearing pig tusks and shells (signs of wealth).

When they arrived at the community of Angeruk, the two related the news of the massacre and how they'd barely escaped.

PICKING UP THE PIECES

Phyliss was cleaning clothes in their Maytag washing machine. The Lord flashed Isaiah 43:2—"When thou passest through the waters I will be with thee"—into her mind. She remembered how this verse had given Elisabeth Elliot strength after her husband Jim's murder.

Suddenly the radio crackled. Excited, Phyliss rushed to it and turned up the volume. She was dismayed to hear the voice wasn't her husband's. The transmission was from Angeruk and in the Dani language. It reported that Stan and Phil had been attacked. The exact word was that the white men were 'hit,' and Phyliss wasn't sure what that meant.

"In Dani it has two meanings: *hit* or *killed*. I hoped it meant that they were alive."

The broken radio meant she couldn't ask for more information. The terrible uncertainty kept her up all night. She told the Lord, "I can't face life without Phil. You know this."

She remembered Stan surviving his arrow wounds and prayed for the same outcome.

That night, an earthquake shook the Masters' home and caused a full bookcase to fall over. Despite that ominous sign, she still believed Phil must be alive. She couldn't accept that he might be dead.

It took weeks to uncover the full truth. Many were involved in the investigation of the murders. A plane piloted by MAF's Paul Pontier and a helicopter flown by Bob Hamilton went out to look for the men's remains.

One of the surviving Dani carriers, Degen, accompanied the team. He helped them locate the site of the killings. They discovered broken arrows, bloodstains, a damaged radio, and bone fragments.

The official report was that the four men had definitely been killed on September 25. They had each been pierced with dozens of arrows.

The news of Stan and Phil's deaths spread like wildfire. For the first time, people around the world were focused on the unknown Yali. Thousands began praying for them and the mourning families.

The confirmation of Phil's death hit Phyliss hard. She escaped to her bedroom to cry. "My main goal was to hold it all together and to carry on for the children."

The three older ones (Crissie, Curtis, and Becky) eventually returned to boarding school, while five-year-old Rob remained at home. Phyliss was three months pregnant with Tim.

A few weeks after Phil's death, as a meal was served, Rob said, "If Daddy was here, he would be sitting at the end of the table."

The comment made her realize how much he missed his father.

Yali woman with load.

Another time Rob was overheard telling a friend, "My daddy is in heaven." The other boy responded, "My baby brother, Gregory, is in heaven, and so they are there together."

Phyliss' twelve-year-old son, Curt, once said, "Daddy never hurt anyone."

She replied, "No, he didn't. That's the wonderful thing about him giving his life."

Crissie was thirteen at the time. "I realized it was difficult and I was affected. But it wasn't a great crisis of faith because of my mother's strong faith. Her conviction of God's calling on her life and her passion that people needed to hear the gospel, helped us through our grief."

Although Phyliss knew that the men had been killed by cannibals, the Lord had permitted this to happen. He brought her key Bible verses such as "Do not fear those who kill the body but cannot kill the soul (Matthew 10:28)" and "Absent from the body is to be present with the Lord (2 Corinthians 5:8)."

The Dales were also grieving. It was not their first experience with sorrow. While still in Australia, Stan and Pat's firstborn had fallen ill. Despite heart-wrenching prayers, he had died. Did they sense, perhaps, it was the first of other losses to come? Just as no answers had come when the baby had died—so none came now.

Wes Dale, who was eleven when his father was murdered, remembers: "My younger brother and I were living in Melbourne, at a home for missionary children. We received a telegram saying Dad was 'missing, believed killed.' I knew right then that Dad had died."

He could imagine his father standing firm and shouting to Phil to run as the first arrows hit. Wes later learned that Phil stayed with Stan and refused to run away.

"It wasn't until December [three months later] that we were able to return to Dutch New Guinea to see Mum."

Years afterward, he spoke with one of the surviving Dani carriers who had accompanied the fateful expedition. "The description of their deaths was horrifying."

Others were also troubled by the murders. David Martin, a missionary to the Dani, remembers: "I was shattered and grieved deeply. I was the first to learn of the killing, by two-way radio, from the mission community at Angeruk. I still remember my weak knees."

Another missionary, John Wilson, was in the United Kingdom preparing to go to Dutch New Guinea when he received a telegram of the deaths.

"I was horrified. I then fully realized the kind of situation I was expecting to serve in."

Three years later, he and his family would be translating the Bible with the Yali.

***

So much sadness. Overwhelming grief. Unanswered questions. The Dutch New Guinea missionary community was asking God, "Why were Stan and Phil killed?"

The new churches at Ninia and Korupun were left without key contacts. Crissie Masters said that "it appeared God's work had suffered a huge blow."

THE PLANE CRASH

MISSIONARIES Gene and Lois Newman were originally from Amity, Oregon. As part of Mission Aviation Fellowship (MAF) they'd relocated to Dutch New Guinea. They spent Christmas Day 1968 at home with their four children: Paul, Steven, Joyce, and Jonathan. Paul fondly remembers stringing garlands of popcorn while baby Jonathan watched all the festivities.

They left the following morning for a week's vacation in the southern part of the country. This included a visit with missionary friends Don and Carol Richardson and their kids.

On the morning of December 31, the Newmans were preparing to spend time in Mulia with the Maynards. Tim Maynard and Paul Newman were best friends and classmates. They had grand plans to build a wooden raft for the nearby fish pond.

MAF pilot Menno Voth picked up the Newmans in a small, single-engine plane. Next to Menno sat Gene Newman with Joyce on his lap. Nine-year-old Paul was directly behind the pilot. His mom, Lois, held baby Jonathan. In the very back was five-year-old Steven. It would be a short flight over the mountains to Mulia.

On the same route two hours earlier, Menno had radioed to another pilot: "It's a beautiful morning, a good day to fly, and I can see the mountain ranges."

Shortly after taking off with the Newmans, the weather suddenly changed for the worse, with monsoon winds blowing from the west. Even on a clear day flying in the mountains was challenging in a Cessna with minimal instruments, but with poor visibility (due to heavy cloud cover) it was extremely hazardous.

Missionary plane taking off in Dutch New Guinea.

Unable to see through the low clouds and steady rain, Menno flew into the Seng Valley instead of the similar Baliem River Valley. He was twenty miles off course and didn't realize it.

Had the clouds been just five hundred feet higher, he could have made a safe 360-degree turn and flown out of the narrow valley.

"It seemed I could have reached out and touched the trees — we were that close to the side of the mountain," recalls Paul Newman.

Seconds later, the plane's right wing hit a tree that was leaning out from the steep mountainside. It sheared off the entire wing. Instantly all the horror of a crashing plane occurred:

screeching-ripping-tumbling-burning-smoking-
gasping-clutching-screaming

The plane Paul was on crashed in the remote mountains of New Guinea on Dec. 31, 1968. The nine-year-old was the only survivor.

The Cessna somersaulted down the mountain, ripping off the left wing. The tail section tore away, and then the nose. The door disappeared. With each jolting hit, aviation fuel spewed everywhere. The cabin—now a shell—came to rest on its right side, blocking the doorway. Fire engulfed the mountainside.

Trapped inside the fuselage, nine-year-old Paul instinctively realized he was the only one alive. With the plane burning, there was no time to think. Desperately, he searched for an exit. The windows were partially flattened by the impact, but he finally found a tiny opening. It was too small for him—he tried it anyway. Miraculously he squeezed through and emerged into the rain. He ran away from the raging fire as fast as his bare feet would take him.

A MYSTERIOUS LOCATION

The confused and grief-stricken boy ran down the steep trail into the valley. He'd lost his glasses and the world was fuzzy. He was lightly dressed, freezing and sopping wet from the rain.

Where am I? Who will help me? he wondered.

Young Paul had no idea that he was near a village of cannibals. These same savages had brutally murdered Stan Dale and Phil Masters just three months before. The missionaries had camped by the very river Paul was about to cross.

The only way over the flowing rapids was by way of a sideless "bridge" of tree limbs tied with pieces of rattan. Paul crawled across on his hands and knees—trying not to look between the gaps at the wild water rushing below. Large rocks amidst the torrential waters would assure a quick death for anyone who fell.

Reaching the end of the bridge, he scrambled up the bank and started running again. *Up, up, keep going, don't stop,* he told himself as he continued to the other side of the rugged valley. After more than an hour of struggle, he collapsed on the plateau.

Suddenly, an unusual figure, wearing dried vines around his abdomen, appeared in the path.

Yet Paul wasn't afraid. He had never even heard of cannibals.

"This odd-looking man slowly approached me. I thought he was like the Dani. Because they were friendly, I had no fear of him."

The stranger gestured for the boy to come, so without any idea of where he was being led, Paul followed. Soon he was in a hut eating sweet potatoes.

This man was Kusoho, a Yali witch doctor. He had argued against killing Phil and Stan. After the murders, the military had come to investigate and he was worried that they'd return with their "boom booms" (guns). So when he saw the *ururu* — the Yali word for *thunder* was what they called an airplane — fall from the

This is the "bridge" that young Paul had to use to reach the Yali village. Here he is crossing an "improved" version on his return visit in 1991.

sky and Paul emerge from the fiery wreck, he wondered if caring for the boy might mend relations.

Hopefully, they will respond to me and my people with forgiveness.

However, no one else wanted anything to do with the child, so Kusoho stayed up all night to keep the fire going. He knew Paul was soaking wet and hoped to warm him.

Meanwhile, missionaries were using three planes to search for survivors. Because of limited daylight hours and the monsoon weather conditions moving in from the west, search and rescue efforts were restricted on the first day. A helicopter from Papua New Guinea was called in to assist, but it would take a day to arrive. Each search plane was assigned a certain area and carried emergency supplies to drop to any survivors.

Paul, Salela (a local chief), and Kusoho in 1991, with the last remaining pieces of the tail section of the plane that crashed in 1968.

"It is extremely difficult terrain, and spotting a downed aircraft was a major challenge," remembers missionary David Martin, who was part of the search. "We received a radio call from another plane that the crash had been spotted, but there was no sign of survivors. We headed to that area. We took a few pictures of the wreckage and returned to Wamena, quite convinced that all had perished."

The missionaries were stunned to learn that the plane had crashed so near the Yali village where Stan and Phil were killed. This created an uncanny feeling—was it only coincidence? Could this disaster somehow be part of God's divine plan?

Paul spent each day sitting on top of a large boulder to get warmth from the sun. He still wore the same wet clothes. He could see the crash site across the valley. Every few hours the search planes would fly into his view. Since Paul had grown up around airplanes he didn't get excited, knowing it was impossible for them to land.

No one on the planes spotted him.

He sobbed constantly. *Will I ever get out of this village?* he wondered.

On the morning of January 2, Paul was on the rock when he saw a helicopter circling above. He realized that it could land in the jungle.

Paul, in 1991, on his return visit to the village where the plane crashed.

He watched it descend in the area of the crash site. Excited, he leaped up, hurdling over rocks as he raced down the steep slope. He ran until he reached the river and began crawling over the primitive "bridge." Halfway across, he saw two missionary men he knew on the other side of the river. They shouted to him: "Stay put! We'll come to you."

Mercifully, this kept Paul from viewing the burned plane and the remains of his family.

The men had come to investigate the crash in person. Seeing the survivor, they radioed for the helicopter to return. Hank asked Paul many questions regarding the final moments of his flight.

On the ride home Paul sat next to Priscilla Voth, the widow of the pilot of the doomed plane. They were able to comfort each other in their common grief.

THE TRUE LORD OF THE EARTH

IT didn't happen overnight, the way anyone would have expected or chosen, but God brought the gospel to the Yali.

Kusoho's remarkable rescue and friendship of Paul became a catalyst for God's powerful love to enter the community. The local Yali chief promised safety, so Dani and Yali Christians came and

Locals worshipping God at the Jubilee.

started ministries. They shared the biblical teachings that Phil and Stan had sacrificed so much to bring.

Today, there are many Yali who followed Kusoho's example and serve the Lord. Kusoho gained acclaim throughout the area and became an influential leader. He died of natural causes in late 2013. Living into his mid-70s is a remarkable feat for members of this primitive culture.

Woman at the Jubilee celebrating the fiftieth anniversary of the arrival of the first missionaries in Ninia.

Paul Newman currently lives in Oregon with his family. In 1991, after 23 years away, he visited with Kusoho and the Yali. He discovered they had been using a wing from his crashed airplane as their communion table. Though he'd only been in Kusoho's care for a few days, everyone still considered him the witch doctor's adopted son, *Babol*.

Dongla remains a committed Christian, teaching the Bible to many.

Pat Dale passed away in 2006. Her son, Wes, serves as a missionary in New Guinea.

Phyliss Masters lived in Dutch New Guinea for another nineteen years. Her son, Tim, was born six months after her husband's death. At age three, the little boy would look through scrapbooks and point out his daddy.

She now lives in her home state of Iowa. Her continued faithfulness to the Lord is a great witness to everyone who meets her.

The key events that God used to reach the Yali were the courageous faith of Dongla, the medicine man's son; the killing of Stan and Phil; the plane crash; and Paul's rescue by a cannibal.

In ways that no one could have imagined, the true Lord of the Earth replaced hatred, fear, and killing, with love.

Phyliss in 2013.

DINO KARTSONAKIS

DINO KARTSONAKIS recorded his first piano album at age seventeen. His professional training was at King's College, the Juilliard School of Music, and at music conservatories in Germany and France. He then toured with Arthur Rubinstein.

He has recorded more than fifty albums. He plays his mixture of classical and sacred music to audiences world-wide, including his Christmas shows in Branson, Missouri. In 2013 he performed at Carnegie Hall for the second time.

Dino has won the "Instrumentalist of the Year" Dove Award seven times. His albums, *Somewhere in Time* and *Classical Peace*, both won Dove Awards.

Develop as fully as we can
the gifts God has given us,
and never stop learning.

Ludwig Beethoven

Small Problems

What is key to a world-class pianist?

BY JEANETTE CHAFFEE

WHEN DINO KARTSONAKIS WAS THREE, HE CAME HOME from church, sat at the piano, and picked out the melody of "At the Cross." He says, "Even at three years of age, children are influenced by musical sounds; just choose whatever you want them to hear."

He does believe in formal training. "Although I wanted to play everything by ear, it was very important for me to become disciplined and learn to read notes. At age seven, I began taking music lessons with a lady from church."

That was also when he accepted Christ. His love of God is still evident throughout his life. "From what I've seen in this world — I couldn't possibly exist without the Lord. I depend on Him for everything. *Everything.*

"Our hope is in Christ Jesus. He is our *only* hope — *not* the things of this world. I stood at the bedside of a young man dying of cancer. I told him, 'I pray your heart is right with the Lord.' We must confess our sins. Ask for forgiveness at the cross of Jesus Christ. He gives life eternal."

Dino emphasizes that we can't depend upon spiritual leaders or personalities. A theme of his ministry has been *turn your eyes upon Jesus.* "That is the key. *Jesus* lifts our burdens. He gives victory through life's problems."

He is glad that a pianist's problems aren't always so serious. Once, his piano bench collapsed. He remembers that "everyone chuckled, but boy did it hurt!"

Another time he came on stage before a capacity crowd. But there was *no piano!* He talked to the audience until it arrived. The crowd thought this was planned.

He's always adored performing. "I love what I do. *I just love it.* I can't wait for the concert. People come up to me afterward and say, 'What you played tonight really blessed me and encouraged me to not give up.'"

Yet, mixed with all the joys, Dino and Cheryl were challenged when their daughter was diagnosed with multiple sclerosis. Another setback was in 2011 when they lost their Missouri home in a flood. His grand pianos, awards, and costumes were all destroyed. He's just grateful that no one in his family was injured. To help his community rebuild after the flood, he performed fundraising concerts.

He also raised money to build a hospital wing in Haiti. He believes that keeping a global perspective is important. In their travels Dino and Cheryl have seen poverty, starvation, homelessness, and even kids dying. It keeps him humble.

"Our problems are small in comparison."

PART 2

MORE
EXTRAVAGANT
GRACES

WHEN YOU THOUGHT
I WASN'T LOOKING

*I saw you hang my
first painting on
the fridge door...*

*I saw you make my
favorite cake just for me...*

*I felt you kiss me
goodnight...*

I heard you say a prayer...

*When you thought I
wasn't looking...*

I was looking even more.

Author Unknown

Tributes

**You've just read their public stories...
Now hear what their families have to say**

SANDRA ALDRICH

A Woman of Faith

BY HOLLY HULEN, DAUGHTER

Extravagant Listening

*The Lord will hear when I
call to Him.*   PSALM 4:3

THE ALARM CLOCK AWAKENS MY MOM, SANDRA ALDRICH, every morning at 6:33 a.m. She has chosen this time to awaken because of the Scripture, "Seek ye first the

195

kingdom of God and His righteousness; and all these things shall be added unto you (Matthew 6:33)."

After shutting off the buzzing alarm, she turns on the lamp by her bed, props a pillow behind her, pulls a shawl around her shoulders, and opens her Bible. She always begins her day by reading God's Word. After her reading, she looks across her bedroom at the dresser lined with framed family photos. Looking at each person, she says an individual prayer.

A year ago, my mom wanted to challenge herself to pray for her loved ones in new ways. She wanted to know what she could be praying for *specifically*. Mom said she always asks God for protection, guidance, and strength, but wanted to know about other needs.

My ten-year-old mentioned how he was frustrated he couldn't make better tackles during his football games and how the coach would yell at him. My six-year-old said he wanted to get better at writing his numbers so he could receive a school award. My husband and I were concerned about career choices that could lead to a family move.

After the four of us told my mom these needs, she seriously said, "Thank you for telling me these requests. I appreciate your trust."

Shouldn't we be thanking her — instead of her thanking us? I wondered.

She often follows up and asks about our concerns so she can update her list. And she reminds me daily of her petitions either through email or a quick voice mail.

My mom's prayers go back to my childhood. She would drive my brother and me to school every morning. She always would say, "Lord, please place your protection around Holly and Jay — in front of them, behind them, over their heads, and under their feet."

If we had an exam at school that day, she would ask God to help us remember what we had studied. She always concluded by saying, "Thank You, Lord, for hearing us. Thank You. We do not pray to air."

These needed prayers continued through my college years. I would call her and express my stress over an upcoming exam or difficult paper I needed to write. After a long conversation affirming that I would write a wonderful paper, study hard, and do well on my exam, she always ended our conversation with an appeal to God.

Before saying good-bye, she would "hug" me through the phone. She would tell me she was placing her arms around my back and then she would make a squeezing sound that usually caused me to laugh. She never hung up without telling me she loved me.

I have now been married for over fifteen years. Not a day goes by without my thanking the Lord for my godly mother. I would not be the woman I am today without her love and much-needed prayers.

My own desire is that my sons look up to me as I do my mom.

...And Another Life Lesson

BY JAY ALDRICH, SON

Extravagant Blessing

Her children arise and call her
blessed. PROVERBS 31:28

THERE ARE DOZENS OF STORIES I COULD TELL ABOUT MOM giving me important life lessons. Some lessons saved me trouble — others would have, had I listened. Once I became (or at least looked like I became) a grown-up, something happened that made me say, "Oh ... that's what Mom was talking about."

When I was a little kid, we had a curio cabinet with shelves full of owls. Some were wooden, some were ceramic, and some were metal. Each was pretty, different, and needed to be dusted.

One day, it dawned on me these things had to come from somewhere, so I asked Mom, "Why do you have a case full of owls?"

She sighed and said, "I once casually mentioned I liked owls. After that, people started buying me little owl statues."

I laughed and said something like, "That's silly." Mom shrugged and responded with a half, "Yeah, I guess" and half, "Keep dusting."

After a move or two, we weren't an easy drive from the people who had given her these owls. We were finally able to sell them at garage sales, donate them to Goodwill, or give them to hapless people who casually mentioned they liked owls.

Years passed. I moved out, married, and bought my own home. We had a little porch on the back, maybe four feet by six, looking at an empty backyard. I made a joke about getting some garden gnomes to yell at, and everybody laughed.

I forgot the comment... until people started buying garden gnomes for me.

Visitors would bring one. I'd go out to dinner with friends and they'd bring one. I'd go over to their house and they'd have one for me. They'd say, "I saw this and thought of you!"

My wife and I have never purchased a garden gnome—and yet, at last count, we've been "blessed" with more than thirty of the things standing around the backyard, looking up at the porch.

Mom, I'm sorry I laughed at your owl collection. Chalk up another life lesson: I had no idea an innocent comment could produce such strange results!

BILL & NANCIE CARMICHAEL

Rooted in Grace

BY CHRISTIAN CARMICHAEL, SON

Extravagant Grace

Be humble and gentle. Be patient with each other, making allowance for each other's faults because of your love. EPHESIANS 4:2

MY MOM AND DAD HAVE BEEN PRAISED IN CERTAIN CIRCLES for having some of the finest parenting skills on the planet. They have written a number of books about how to parent effectively. They have held hundreds of seminars where they taught current and would-be parents the best ways to usher children into adulthood using a combination of white-knuckled prayers, psychological tactics, and unholy amounts of patience.

I was one of the five kids upon which they practiced their craft. As the middle child (I preferred "center child"), it was my self-appointed job to pay careful attention and take notes so that later, when they were rich and famous, I could write the best-selling tell-all that would lay our secrets bare and maybe even inspire a gritty Hollywood production or two.

That didn't happened because my parents just never held hypocrisy well. When they made a mistake, they admitted it, asked for forgiveness, and even used it as a teaching lesson.

For someone growing up among the televangelist scandals of the 1980s, I kept waiting for some big, nasty secret to burst out and ruin my parents' reputations—forcing them to find a new line of work, probably in accounting or farming.

Instead, Dad and Mom sought grace through every stumble—for each other, for their children, for their friends, for anyone, including people in town who didn't like them because of their faith.

My parents are not perfect, of course. Dad threatened our lives when he discovered we were using his framed safari photos as a literal dartboard. (I now understand with perfect clarity why he was so upset.) I also recall Mom skidding our van to a stop some-where along a dusty highway in Wyoming to whip us with a tree branch (we were preteens snapping each other with rubber bands and howling).

Later on, we laughed about these memories, and many more like them. They actually drew us closer as a family—like shared combat stories. And later, when real wounds came—such as those from a rebellious child or a betrayal caused by close friends—my parents remained rooted in grace that surpasses all understanding. I suppose that's why they call grace *amazing*.

More than anything, Dad and Mom have taught me that it's never too late to apply a little forgiveness to someone else, or even yourself. Doing so allows God to turn ugly moments into beautiful examples of how His grace wins.

And *that's* a legacy worth writing about.

Loving in Spite of Differences

BY AMY CARMICHAEL CAVIGGIA, ADOPTED DAUGHTER

Extravagant Never-Failing Love

Love suffers long and is kind ... [Love]
bears all things, believes all things,
hopes all things.   1 CORINTHIANS 13:4, 7

GROWING UP IN THE HOME OF BILL AND NANCIE CARMICHAEL, I had difficulty fitting into a culture that was so different from my orphanage in Korea. Looking back now, I would not change a thing.

My parents showed me love and grace just by being there, no matter what. They came to my basketball and volleyball games. They stuck by me in the hardest times and made me feel included, just as they did with my four brothers.

Mom and Dad learned to accept me as I was, and I learned to accept them as they were. I'm very thankful for my childhood.

JEANETTE CHAFFEE

Unforgettable

BY MONICA PLATA, NIECE

Extravagant Generosity

*Do good, be rich in helping
others.*   1 TIMOTHY 6:18

CHRISTMAS 2005 IS MY FAVORITE MEMORY OF AUNT JEANETTE. My brother and sister and I *loved* getting mail. We each received our own beautifully decorated envelope from Aunt Jeanette. I felt very important. What could be inside? We were itching with anticipation but we had to wait until Christmas.

A note read: "No peeking! Open all of these at the same time."

Curiosity got the best of me. A gift card? Movie passes? Starbucks? (Aunt Jeanette loves her coffee!)

Mom made us wait until we'd unwrapped all our other big, elaborate presents before we could see what was in the small envelopes. When it was finally time, we simultaneously opened them. I was stunned: *the gifts were not for us!*

We each received a photo illustrating a World Vision donation given in our honor to needy children somewhere in the world. We went around our family circle, taking turns displaying the pictures of our gifts and reading our personalized messages. A stuffed lamb and Bible story books from Hannah, and two soccer balls from Ryan.

He read his inscription out loud: "Many homeless orphans come to World Vision children's centers to play. The kids love soccer, but most have to use makeshift balls made from wads of trash."

Wads of trash? What a shock. We lived an affluent lifestyle in the California Bay Area. I never imagined this.

As for my gift? I "received" a *goat!* My note said: "A goat provides a family with fresh milk, cheese, and added income."

It was beyond wonderful.

It reminded me of the true meaning of Christmas: God gave His best gift—His Son, Jesus—to be the Savior to a hurting world.

The years have flown by and my aunt's envelopes continue. Each time I am touched beyond words.

Christmas 2011 brought special memories. My husband and I had only been married about a year. Merging all the events to include both families brought joy: the traditional Christmas Eve dinner at Mom's house, a midnight church service with my husband's family, and Christmas gift opening.

I sat alone, enjoying the quiet, petered out from all the great festivities. Leaning back on the couch to relax, I reached for Aunt Jeanette's annual present. *What is she "giving" me this year?*

Clean water! She had me helping to build a well. The picture featured water flowing from a spout. The World Vision card explained: "Some children have to drink disease-infested water… A clean well cuts a child's mortality rate in half."

I was teary-eyed. *Did I tell her about my water problem in Honduras?* I was sure I hadn't.

I recalled the summer I was fourteen and joined a missions group in Honduras. Aunt Jeanette supported me in this endeavor.

Each group member had been given a canteen to hold our filtered drinking water. Unfortunately, mine became contaminated by horse manure. No matter what I did, I couldn't get the smell out, even though the bottle was disinfected. No extra containers were available. I became desperate.

We rode horseback every day in the scorching sun, visiting villages and telling people about Jesus. It was horribly hot in our boots and long pants. Water was rationed. Fortunately, my kind teammates shared their water with me since I didn't have any.

I can't imagine daily life for people in these countries. I saw firsthand the importance of clean drinking water. It's easy for me to take this for granted when I can just turn on a faucet.

Until I wrote this tribute, Aunt Jeanette knew nothing of my incident in Honduras. God directed her to donate priceless water in my name. How wonderful it was for me to receive a gift meant for someone else!

DONNIE DEE

My Obedient Servant Leader

BY JOHNNY DEE, SON

Extravagant Service

Hate what is wrong. Stand on the side of the good ... take delight in honoring each other. ROMANS 12:9–10

EVERY DAY WHEN I CAME HOME—FROM SCHOOL, PLAYING basketball, or somewhere else—Dad would ask me the same question: "Were you a leader today?"

When I was young, I didn't really understand what he meant.

Dad exemplified self-sacrifice and honoring others. He always challenged me by saying, "Being a leader means being different. Did you stand up for what you believed in today? Being a man means you must have character." He continued by warning me that "many fall into temptation."

Many times when I was enticed to lie, cheat, or be disrespectful to someone, I thought of Dad and chose to do the right thing. I didn't want to disappoint him when I got home.

I'm in my twenties now and attending college. On the weekends, there's partying and drinking. I don't participate.

Looking back on what Dad taught me, I now see why it's so important to be motivated to please the Lord all the time. I praise God for giving me a dad who always points me to Jesus. He loves and serves others. My family lives by biblical principles, including: not cheating, not lying, being nice to people, and loving others more than yourself. I can honestly say my dad is a 24/7 Christian.

When I was eleven or twelve years old, Dad started the Shadow Ridge Knights, a support group of fathers and sons. Shadow Ridge is the name of the community where we live. We would get together every couple of months — both Christians and non-Christians. I knew these boys from sports, school, or church.

(Now, over eight years later, we still get together. Since my friends and I have finished high school, we've gone different directions. I love that we still meet, even though it's only about once a year now.)

At our Shadow Ridge Knights meetings, Dad would share about important virtues such as honesty, servitude, sacrifice, and courage. After our discussions, we would have an outing to illustrate that particular virtue.

For example, after talking about honesty, we went golfing: no cheating or lying — even if no one would find out you nudged the ball or claimed less strokes.

For serving others, we went to Mexico and built a house for charity. For an explanation of sacrifice, Dad took our group to a naval base where we heard an officer talk about his experiences fighting for freedom.

When I was eleven, to demonstrate courage, we took turns flying in a single-engine prop plane—just big enough for the pilot and two passengers. My friend was chosen to be the copilot. Boy, was I nervous!

My father is amazing. I've witnessed the impact he has on people. I see the way he invests his time. He always makes himself available. He never rushes discussions with my friends, coaches, or me. He listens carefully.

He's always sharing God's story. I recently received the greatest text message of my life. My sixth grade basketball coach—my father had faithfully kept in touch with him—became a Christian with Dad that day! Coach said witnessing our family's behavior over the years made him curious about the God that we serve.

This was so much like when my dad accepted the Lord through the influence of his teammates.

My goal in life is to glorify Christ—not myself. God will bless my obedience. I'm reminded of what Corrie ten Boom said: "Don't bother to give God instructions; just report for duty."

Like my dad, that's what I do.

ELISABETH ELLIOT

A Regal Lady

BY CHRISTIANA R.S. GREENE, THIRD GRANDCHILD

Extravagant Obedience and Forgiveness

I delight to do Your will oh my God ...
With You there is forgiveness.   PSALM 40:8, 130:4

I PUT MY GRANDMOTHER, ELISABETH ELLIOT, ON A PEDESTAL. I thought I could never measure up, because she was so disciplined and full of grace. All aspects of her life demonstrated her obedience to God and forgiveness to others. I felt I had the opposite of these qualities. *How can she love me?* I thought. *She's a kind, godly woman and I'm not as ladylike or as quiet as I should be.*

I was Granny's third grandchild. She taught me to play the piano correctly, focusing on the gentle strains of hymns such as "Be Still my Soul" or "We Rest on Thee." She instructed, "Let your left hand play softer than your right, which plays the melody."

How I loved our walks together. We'd climb down the rocky coastline near her home in Massachusetts and collect mussels. She'd steam them and serve them with hot butter. They were yummy!

Food at Granny's was always wonderful. She prepared Earl Grey tea and fed me her delicious vegetable or tomato soup. I loved her special treats of ice cream. We'd laugh over funny lines from movies like "Singing in the Rain." She could quote everyone from Winnie the Pooh to St. Augustine.

Granny was sweet and funny and delightful. She could be firm and direct, but she was always patient. She was reserved and did her hair in a bun. We girls were expected to wear clean skirts. She taught me how to be feminine, "approved unto God" as her husband—my Grandpa Jim—once said.

When I got the opportunity to hear my Granny speak publicly, I always sat listening in amazement. Such poise and elegance! She had so much wisdom about loneliness, the faithfulness of God, and the gift of singleness.

I am eternally grateful for the many huge and tiny life lessons she taught me. She was always patient (even with children who interrupted her). The way she washed dishes, did the laundry, and ironed were unique: she would sing—happy tunes by Johnny Cash or Patsy Cline, or hymns such as "Jesus is All the World to Me"—the entire time.

I never got to see or know my Grandpa Jim. One day I asked Granny, "How could you go live with Grandpa's killers in the jungle?"

Her instant response: "It was God's will. All to His glory!"

With these words, Granny taught me her most important lesson: *she forgave the unthinkable.*

My Irreplaceable Namesake

BY ELISABETH S. MARTIN, SECOND GRANDCHILD

Extravagant Patience

A person's wisdom yields patience. PROVERBS 19:11

I WAS NAMED AFTER ELISABETH ELLIOT, MY GRANDMOTHER. SHE was keen on order, discipline, and routine. From her I learned how to iron a shirt, hang clothes on a line, and polish silver until I could see my face in it.

She would answer every note I sent to her and was interested in what I had been doing in school, what kind of weather we'd been having, and what sewing projects I had going. I often sent her my essays so that she could read and comment on them.

Granny loved to sing. Every time I heard her, I felt the presence of Jesus. She taught me to play hymns. Some of her favorites were "The Wonderful Grace of Jesus," "Near the Cross," and "Great is Thy Faithfulness." If I was playing, she would direct. If *she* was at the piano, I had to be standing next to her turning the pages and singing.

Despite being deluged with piles of mail, Granny read every letter — even the ones that were twelve pages long! She was so generous with her valuable time.

After her speaking engagements, there was always a long line for autographs. I felt it was too much, but she never rushed people. She was just the same at home.

I remember her wonderful picnic lunches. Each ham, cheese, or egg salad sandwich was on homemade bread and wrapped tightly in wax paper. I loved her freshly baked snickerdoodles and oatmeal raisin cookies. She would serve me tea, using her fine English bone china. I felt like a princess!

Granny's words were always wise. When I was an easily distracted young girl, she told me: "Keep your mind on one thing until you get it done. Only when it's done do you move on to something else."

In my teen years, she counseled, "Keep boys at arm's length. Keep your clothes on."

Faithfulness in little things was a principle she repeated over and over. These weren't just words — she lived them. I will always be challenged by her example.

VALERIE ELLIOT SHEPARD

To My Lovely Mama

BY CHRISTIANA R.S. GREENE, DAUGHTER

Extravagant Servant's Heart

She gets up while it is still dark. She provides food for her family. PROVERBS 31:15

The lady who walks in beauty and grace,
the woman who is strong and trusts God

The female whom I call Mama, the
role that I someday hope to be

The girl who was a lil' Ecuadorian butterfly

The gal who stole my daddy's heart
thirty-five-plus years ago

The sweet, endearing, cheerful singer,
who taught me to wake up early,
read God's Word and sing hymns

The woman who harmonized to the
Carpenters and other folksingers

The one who texts me prayers and
verses and speaks around the globe

The person who taught me to love
classical literature and write

Now the mother with an empty nest
who embraces four grandchildren, three
sons-in-law and two daughters-in-law!

Thank you for showing me
things like cooking and cleaning,
loving and living well!

PHYLISS MASTERS

Home

BY CRISSIE MASTERS RASK, DAUGHTER

Extravagant Strength

*Strength and dignity are her clothes and
she smiles at the future.* PROVERBS 31:25

WHEN OUR FAMILY FIRST MOVED TO DUTCH NEW GUINEA, we were assigned to Karubaga. This was a mission station in the beautiful Swart (now Toli) Valley. Our house had been built by another missionary. It was an aluminum roofed, split-board-sided home with a wood cooking stove, a bucket shower, and woven bamboo walls.

I have happy memories of that house.

Mom worked diligently to learn the local Dani language, homeschool us kids, and train Dani helpers to cook. Mom and Dad came from farming backgrounds and both were resourceful. They ordered vegetable and flower seeds and even fruit trees from Australia and planted them around our yard. Dad was always making practical improvements to our house.

Their passion was teaching the Dani, who were turning to follow Christ in amazing numbers. They felt God calling them to reach out to other valleys, open an airstrip, and move our family to an unreached area much farther to the east. Dad hiked the treacherous seven days beyond Ninia—where fellow missionaries Stan and Pat Dale lived among the Yali—to Korupun. There he built an airstrip so our family could move to the Kimyal tribe. We had to learn their language to teach them about Jesus.

I bugged Mom about leaving the beautifully simple home in Karubaga. I would miss the fruit trees and the flowers, and the running water Dad had cleverly piped through the wood stove to heat it.

I clearly remember her response that the Kimyal people still had not heard about Jesus. We must go, not with reluctance, but with confidence that Korupun would also become our home. We would be happy wherever God wanted us to be.

Our first home at Korupun had a thatched roof and burlap bags lining the inside walls. Part of the house had dirt floors, and the rest consisted of rough bark floors. The outhouse was down the path.

Dad eventually built a low fence around our house to keep people from poking holes to see through the glassine windows. Bows and arrows had to be left outside the fence at a sort of "hitching post." Some people were rowdy and hotheaded. Once, in our yard, someone was shot through the hand.

The fact that we kids did not feel this lifestyle was a huge sacrifice, or even out of the ordinary, I credit to Mom's ability to bloom where she was planted and serve the Lord with courage and true gladness.

In addition to teaching Bible and literacy, our parents were constantly improving our home. Dad brought in goats, planted plum trees, and made fishponds. Mom grew roses and gladioli. They handed out vegetable and peanut seeds for the Dani to grow so they could improve their diet. Eventually, Dad built a larger wood house with a stone fireplace.

When my father was killed, we had to leave behind the house he'd so lovingly built. As God would have it, we moved back to Karubaga into the same house I hadn't wanted to leave.

In Karubaga Mom could be part of an established ministry, in a community with other missionaries, and carry on the work to which she had been called. She had to relearn the Dani language so she could teach the Bible.

Over time, as our grief eased, our home again became a place of warmth and hospitality. Mom taught Dani helpers to make bread, fried oatmeal, the *best* cinnamon rolls, and other meals. This allowed her to continue her ministry.

I wondered how Mom did it. Not just physically, but emotionally, with joy and not bitterness. She was obedient to the call of God on her life. She was compelled to take the gospel to those who had never heard it, and that did not change when Dad was killed.

Her deep knowledge of God's Word gave her the conviction that God *will* keep His promises, *will* give us strength, and *will* comfort us.

From the time Mom accepted Jesus as her Savior, she has continually made choices based on His love for her. She has responded with obedience. She walks and serves joyfully, even when faced with circumstances far more difficult than leaving behind a house and garden.

God's Restorative Grace

BY JARRET MCCLAIN, SON

Extravagant Restoration

*I will give you back what you lost to
the swarming locusts.* JOEL 2:25

WHEN I WAS FOUR, I DIDN'T KNOW ANYTHING WAS WRONG with our family. Dad chose to sing at nightclubs near our home in North Hollywood so he could be close to us. I remember standing in the back of The China Trader, watching him perform. I understood this was his job.

My favorite time of day was the wee hours of the morning, when Dad returned home. Every night I listened for his 1974 Corvette to pull up in the driveway. He'd come into my bedroom, sit on the edge of the bed, and we'd spend a little time talking together. I felt loved and important.

Dad promised me regular time together. I was excited. However, he sometimes didn't show up. *Where's Daddy? He promised he'd come. Doesn't he love me anymore?*

To cope with my disappointment, I learned not to place too much value in what he said. I told myself, "If he comes home, that'll be great."

Sometimes I saw Mom crying. I also noticed our refrigerator was sometimes bare. Food bags would be left at our front door. People began giving me school clothes.

Many nights over the next eight years, my father didn't come home. Even when he showed up, he no longer came by my room for our "wee hour talks."

About this time, Mom discovered Dad had a terrible cocaine habit. By the time I was age eight, she had quit daily show business to take care of me. She began teaching at Village Christian, where I attended. I loved riding to school with her. On the way, we prayed that God would deliver Dad from his drug addiction.

"Dear Jesus, bring Daddy home," I always prayed.

One day, right after praying this, I saw a police car parked at our house. Three policemen brought my father to the door. "Look, Mommy, God answered my prayer. He brought Daddy home!"

Mom and I attended a weekly Bible study at Church On The Way. Others in the group were also getting through hard times, which encouraged my mom. I loved this—at age five, I had fourteen adults "adopting" me.

We had a guest house behind our home. Jeff, a young Christian man, rented it one summer. Sometimes Mom invited him to have dinner with us. We hung around together. He played the harmonica, and took me to the movies.

Without a dad around much, the Bible study group and Jeff were God's way of shielding and protecting me by His grace.

In 1985, our family hit rock bottom. The nurse at school spoke to my mom. "I've been reviewing Jarret's eye history. His eyes are rapidly getting worse. Something is wrong. You need to see a doctor."

Dad happened to be around and took me to our physician, who told us we needed to see a specialist. We soon received an appointment with Dr. Rosenbaum at the UCLA Eye Institute.

After examining me, Dr. Rosenbaum said: "Jarret is in an advanced stage of an incurable disease known as 'lazy eye syndrome.' He could go blind because his brain isn't using his right eye. He needs surgery—maybe more than once—and he will always wear glasses. The surgery he must undergo is the least likely to succeed."

This medical procedure was in the experimental stages. Lasik had not yet been invented; surgeries were only performed with scalpels. Dr. Rosenbaum accepted me into this testing program.

This health scare was a revelation for my father. He later told me that God said to him, "It's not your son's vision that's the problem. It's you."

When we got home from the doctor's office, Dad explained to Mom, "We're going to have to help Jarret with eye exercises twice a day for six months."

Mom stopped him. "No, not 'we.' *You*. You need to step up to be Daddy."

This meant less going out for my dad. He had to get up very early every day to help me with my exercises before I left for school. Then, every evening before my bedtime, we repeated the routine.

Dad would still slip out to do cocaine, thinking no one would find out. Every time he did this, I lost ground. It never failed. When Dad went out, my eyes deteriorated. When he stayed home, I improved.

Finally, Dr. Rosenbaum threatened to take me out of the program. Dad immediately stopped sneaking out and I made rapid progress.

In June 1986, I had the proposed surgery. For the next three months, Dad and I continued my eye exercises. We started every session with prayer. During this period, the most strenuous physical activity I was permitted was a brisk walk. Any sudden movement or jolting could result in blindness. As a lively eleven-year-old, I loved sports, so that summer was miserable.

Dad promised me, "Anything *you* can't do this summer, I won't do either." When our family and friends took camping trips and everyone else went boating and swimming, Dad remained behind with me. He kept his promise.

That fall, Dr. Rosenbaum ran all kinds of tests. He called in other doctors. Five times they performed the same tests. They whispered among themselves and we didn't know what to think.

My father took control of the situation and asked, "You're scaring my son. What's going on?"

"There's nothing to be scared about," Dr. Rosenbaum said. "Something happened. According to all of our tests, Jarret now has 20/15 vision. It doesn't make sense."

I said, "I told you, Dad. I knew the Lord would heal me."

Dr. Rosenbaum said, "I really do believe that your God is that powerful, because that's the only explanation for what I'm looking at."

Years later, when I was thirty-four, my vision was still 20/20. When I explained my eye problems to the doctor, he said, "You don't wear contacts or glasses. I've only ever heard of one other case like yours."

Dad went off cocaine cold turkey. He had to *want* to do it and turn to God. It wasn't easy for him. Cravings and the jitters still existed, and he slept a lot.

Fortunately, God allows us to be imperfect people. You can't go too far away from Him. He will always say, *"Welcome back."*

Any distance. Any problem. It's inconsequential to God. He promises He will restore — and not partway. True to God's Word, He restored my dad completely.

DON & CAROL RICHARDSON

Stargazing With Dad

BY SHANNON RICHARDSON, SECOND SON

Extravagant Creation

*The heavens are telling the glory of
God; they are a marvelous display of
His craftsmanship.*   PSALM 19:1

EVER SINCE MY YEARS AS A CHILD IN THE DEEP, DARK JUNGLES of New Guinea, the glow of celestial bodies in the night sky has captured my imagination. Many a night, with my tiny hand in Dad's for reassurance, I stood on the footbridge he built over the Tumdu River, getting lessons in what he called "worshiping God." Sometimes we talked for hours; other times we remained very still and silent.

I may not have exactly grasped what worship was, but with burning meteorites streaking earthward, colorful planets, and glowing star fields, I learned the heavens are alive with mind-blowing wonders! I loved sitting close to Dad and experiencing these moments together.

We'd hear the mating calls of crickets reverberating through the damp air: nature's music, still as soothing to me as Simon and Garfunkel's "Sounds of Silence."

The hymns of nature are just what one needs on days when you doubt that the Creator is in control. When personal agonies or accusatory words persist — my faith wears down a little.

But I have a firm foundation. I am deeply thankful for my earthly dad showing me—by example—how to worship and trust my heavenly Father.

I sense He is physically there, just like my dad has always been. The words "Yes, I care," whisper in the darkness, reassuring me. Then I remember Dad and me "worshiping God." When I get afraid or worn down, I feel him holding my hand again.

On Top of the World

BY VALERIE RICHARDSON POWERS, DAUGHTER

Extravagant Beauty

Great are the works of the Lord;
they are pondered by all who
delight in them. PSALM 111:2

MY EIGHT-YEAR-OLD HAZEL EYES WERE WIDE WITH wonder as the mini aircraft flew toward the mountain village of Karubaga. The landscape spread out like a green quilt far below. The roar of the plane engine did not drown out my excitement for this adventure. I was returning to my birth village, a place I hadn't visited since I was a baby.

I had been enjoying new experiences exploring communities all over Papua, Indonesia, where my parents, Don and Carol Richardson, had been missionaries. Every moment of this trip I had been discovering a new world. The sights, sounds, smells, and feel of these cultures were unlike anything I'd encountered in my comfortable Southern California life. I soaked it all up like only a trusting child can do.

I couldn't have chosen a better age to return to the land of my birth. I was young enough to have an open mind, an easy-going attitude, and resiliency against the difficulties, yet I was old enough to remember each experience and emotion. Even at that age, I wanted to preserve each moment forever. I had heard about this place many times from my parents and three older brothers, but I had always felt like an outsider.

Although I had spent the first two years of my life in Papua, I had no memory of it. This trip was enabling me to relate to the cultural heritage the rest of my family valued. I was about to see where I first came into the world.

The village grew closer as the plane descended and finally landed on a dirt airstrip. My parents and I were surrounded by smiling villagers. Strangers would touch our face, hair, and arms as they jumped up and down, exploding with joy. Their boundless enthusiasm was contagious.

The little village was practically built on the side of a mountain. There were steps all over, and you were always looking either up or down. The small buildings and the people flowed with their natural surroundings instead of dominating or fighting them. The picture was beautiful, graceful, and unique.

Next we visited the local hospital, where I had the quirky experience of climbing onto the bed where I was born.

Mom and I walked to the highest point of the village and stopped, transfixed. Below us were rolling hills and valleys as far as the eye could see. We were on top of the world. Tears welled in Mom's eyes and she wore a look of peace and joy. She said, "This is the most beautiful view on earth. I am so blessed to be here sharing God's creation with you. This country will always feel like home to me."

I knew immediately that this moment would be tucked away to treasure forever. Before this, I had not truly appreciated her love for the people of Indonesia. When I saw the joy in her eyes and heard the warmth in her voice, I understood her heart as never before. Her years in Indonesia had not just been a duty that she endured. She was passionate about the life to which God had called her. I was so privileged to share the experience of the land she loved.

In that moment, on top of the world, I felt a bond with her that I will remember for all eternity.

Saving Me From Carl

BY SHANNON RICHARDSON, SECOND SON

Extravagant Protection

The Lord is faithful, and He will strengthen and protect you from the evil one. 2 THESSALONIANS 3:3

WHEN I WAS A TEENAGER, I EARNED A FEW HUNDRED dollars mowing the lawn for a neighbor. Carl sold household cleaning products to stores around Los Angeles. It was evident that his psychological state had unraveled long before I stumbled into his path. He wasn't able to hold a proper job, and this salesman fling wasn't producing much income. He also had a teenage drug addict living in his house and marijuana plants growing in cartons in his backyard.

One day, after I pruned his shrubs, I mentioned that my father, Don Richardson, was a Christian minister. Carl chimed in, "I am a member of the Community Calvary Church in Sierra Madre!"

A Christian? Was that to be believed? I hardly swallowed it. However, the following Sunday, Carl appeared at Lake Avenue Congregational Church. He slipped into the service and sat alone in the balcony, with his dark sunglasses protectively donned. This became routine.

I sat with Carl in the balcony one Sunday. When I ventured into the men's room after the service, he followed me and stood there grinning. *Strange,* I thought.

Striving to gain acceptance as a family friend, he met my mother. She graciously thanked him for the employment he'd given me. He nodded, blushing nervously.

Christmas was approaching. Carl pried me with questions regarding my personal hobbies. I mentioned that I liked music and played guitar.

Not long afterward, he made a first-ever appearance at my home. Carl politely delivered an expensive new electric guitar and small amplifier into the hands of my bewildered mother.

Mom had met Carl at church, but never had reason to suspect anything. Suddenly, she noticed Carl's presence and questioned me. "Just what are you doing with this man to instigate his elaborate gifts? Does he have a family? How much time do you spend with him?"

I answered her questions honestly, but I was too embarrassed to mention the uncomfortable way Carl would put his arm around me at times. We both agreed that he seemed too involved in my life, to the point of becoming intrusive. She advised that I not encourage his generosity any further.

One afternoon, I found my father in the living room. Dad was a well-known Christian author and in demand throughout the world as a conference speaker. It wasn't often I caught him with his feet up, watching TV.

I sat on the couch and made sure I got his full attention. I told him about Carl, his staring, and the touching incidents. I also explained the awkward feeling the gifts gave me. "He is a member of the Community Calvary Church in Sierra Madre," I commented.

Dad's blood boiled.

He darted past me to the phone, snatched it off the hook, and called the Community Calvary Church's office. The youth pastor picked up the line. A long conversation ensued, and an alarming picture of Carl emerged.

He was a convicted sexual predator, and after some "strictly confidential" incidents with youth at the church, he had been instructed by the pastors to stay away.

My dad immediately called the police to confirm this report. They ran a criminal check on Carl. "He's an ex-felon," the officer warned. "He has convictions for sexual molestation. He's out on parole. Instruct your son to have nothing to do with him."

I wondered what my dad would do next.

"Shannon," he instructed me sternly, "I want you to get on the phone and call Carl. Use the calmest, friendliest voice you can. I don't want him to suspect anything. Thank him for all the attention and gifts and ask him to come over here. Tell him I'd like to meet him to thank him personally. Now!"

Carl was surprised by my phone call. He gullibly agreed to come over, probably thinking my dad wanted to discuss the upcoming "camping trip." But he was walking straight into our setup. This time, others were setting the trap, not him.

My father, the tallest and sternest I'd ever seen, faced our unsuspecting visitor. "Carl, get out of Shannon's life. He wants nothing more to do with you. Get lost. I mean it!"

There was a long pause. We watched the words sink in. Carl's face turned pale. His whole body began to shake. His muscles quivered.

Then my dad dealt the knockout punch I wasn't expecting.

"In fact, it would be best if you moved out of this neighborhood. I'm putting the word out about you to the families around here who have children. You'd best be gone from all of our lives very soon. You're the kind of predator we don't want around. Now get off my porch this instant!"

My father's speech ended in a thunderous crescendo, with his fists balled at his sides as if he was about to deliver a Mike Tyson right hook.

The man spun in utter disbelief. He shuffled like a duck down the walk, struggled into his car, and sped off out of sight. That was the end of Carl. His house was empty the next day. He vanished like a ghost, abandoning everything he owned.

I'm so grateful God gave me parents who were attentive and took decisive action to protect me from the evil one.

Extravagant Quotes

SANDRA ALDRICH

"Honey, when you get married, *talk* to your husband. Remember: men read newspapers — not minds."

"Build bridges. Don't burn them."

"Never say the 'D' word, divorce. We need to live with commitment to God that we are going to stay together."

"I don't believe people ever get *over* grief. They get *through* it."

STEPHEN ARTERBURN

"I continue to be surprised by God's grace every day."

"Never give up."

BILL AND NANCIE CARMICHAEL

"The significant promises you make in your life are really the milestones by which you measure your life."

"It takes two to have a marriage. If one person isn't committed, you don't have a marriage."

JEANETTE CHAFFEE

"There are times when no one knows the fear and pain you're experiencing. In those secret moments, Jesus is there. Always has been. Always will be. While carrying His cross to His death, Jesus was *thinking of you*. He understands."

HENRY CLOUD

Best-Selling Author and Speaker

"Come out of darkness, alienation, pain. Come out of your setting and get in with good, loving people and begin to 'reconstruct.' It's called sanctification and changes that heal. We learn how to do what we didn't do earlier. That's how character problems are resolved. It's not about 'dealing with the past.' It can be corrected today."

"Come into new situations to learn new ways. Repent. Agree. Turn from it. Start changing and living in new ways."

"Some adults see others and say 'Wow! I wish I was like that.' The reason they aren't is because the others—like Peter—got wet. He fixed his eyes on Jesus, got up, and tried one more time."

"Information in the head is knowledge. Information in the heart is love. The difference is about eight inches between the head and the heart."

"The process of grief and sadness is God's way of getting rid of things. Grieving is a relational thing with others who understand us."

"When we leave God, we leave life."

"The message of the Bible is that God is looking for you to fix the damage. In terms of hope, it doesn't matter what's happened to you. Jesus came to seek and save that which was lost. In the Greek, the word *lost* means 'fix the damage.'"

"Rebuilding our connectedness means learning how to respond to love and not move away from it."

SHIRLEY DOBSON

"My mother is one of the greatest love gifts in my life."

"I believe with all my heart that prayer and fasting for America is our only hope."

"We want to be good stewards. We don't want to do something stupid in our ministry."

"There's *no* limit to what God will do!"

ELISABETH ELLIOT

"The cross does not exempt us from pain. It transforms us. We give Him our losses, He gives us gain. We give Him our sins, He gives us His righteousness. We bring Him our sorrows, He gives us joy. That's what Christianity is all about."

"It's not explanations that you really need when you're lonely. Your deepest heart needs a relationship with Jesus Christ. He is there."

"I believe the real key of healing is acceptance."

"It makes a tremendous difference to know that Jesus Christ is there in your hospital room, in that lonely kitchen or whatever your horrifying situation is. I'm here to say: *you are not alone.* You are loved. He died for you. He wants to give you joy. That's what the cross is all about."

"There are two things that help me with loneliness and death. They are:
— I'm not alone (Isaiah 42).
— God loves me. He is there."

"The cross is all about transformation. C.S. Lewis said, 'Joy is a serious business.'"

"There are two kinds of loneliness: solitude and aloneness."

"I can testify that in the darkest place, that very thing itself can be transformed into a gateway of joy."

"God is not going to answer our questions necessarily. But He does answer us with Himself. It is not an explanation; it is a relationship. It is not an explanation that you really need. Your deepest heart needs a relationship with Jesus Christ. And He's there. He's waiting for you to turn to Him."

"When people ask me, 'How do I know what the Lord's will is?' I tell them, 'Do the next thing.'"

"Psalm 23 says, 'The Lord is my Shepherd.' You are not alone. None of us is alone."

ALAN HLAVKA

Lead Pastor of Good Shepherd Church

"Daily experience the extravagant love of the Father and give it away to the next person you meet."

DON RICHARDSON

"It is not our gifts and our courage that kept us in cannibal territory in Irian Jaya with an eight-month-old baby son. It was the peace of God that sustained our hearts and minds."

EVELYN SAINT JIMENEZ

Niece of Nate Saint, one of the five missionary martyrs in Ecuador

"A battle seems to be the norm before a great victory. Have peace. Keep marching ahead. Perseverance is faith in the long run."

DAVID STOOP

"Forgiveness can happen without reconciliation. Reconciliation cannot happen without forgiveness."

BARBARA YOUDERIAN

Wife of Roger, one of the five missionary martyrs in Ecuador

"I'm looking forward to seeing my Auca friends in heaven."

An Extravagant Invitation

For all have sinned and come short of the glory of God.
ROMANS 3:23

For the wages of sin is death, but the gift of God is eternal life through Jesus Christ our Lord. **ROMANS 6:23**

For by grace are you saved through faith, and that not of yourselves; it is the gift of God, not of works, lest anyone should boast. **EPHESIANS 2:8-9**

I am the way, the truth, and the life. No man comes to the Father but by Me. **JOHN 14:6**

I stand at the door and knock. If anyone hears My voice and opens the door, I will come in. **REVELATION 3:20**

God has given us eternal life, and this life is in His Son. He who has the Son has life; He who does not have the Son of God does not have life. **1 JOHN 5:11-12**

Acknowledgments

TO all who graciously entrusted your life experiences with me, I am deeply grateful.

Jim Yost and John Wilson—your explanations of the Auca (Waorani) and Yali cultures, respectively, brought them to life.

Wendy Wolfe, Bonny Nickens, Les and Gloria Rivera, Cathy Martorano, Peggy Tank, Larry Hank, Carol Van Wagner, Penny Koffler, Patty Dumdeang, Linda Bradley, Evelyn Jimenez, and Sally Timm—all of your proof-reading eyes went beyond the call of duty.

Lynn Saint, Joe and Susy Saint, Wes Dale, David Martin, Bill Dolan, Doug Steward, Troy Bosteder, Jonathan Peterson, Elizabeth Carras, Paul Powers, Susie Weaver, Arlene Kampmann, Karen Ray, Elaine Evans, Cornelia Flynn, Elvira Monteferrante, Pam Benjamin, and Joy Smith—accolades for your heart-felt support.

The Westbow Press team of Krystal Vincent, Kelli Maxwell, Nate Best, and Andrew Carter—thanks for your expertise and patience.

Marc Zeedar—my fabulous graphic artist, cover and interior designer, and editor-in-chief extraordinaire. Such creativity! You are simply brilliant.

I couldn't have done it without all of you.

Most importantly—thanks to Jesus Christ, my Inspirer of Ideas, who makes dreams a reality.

About the Author

JEANETTE CHAFFEE was sitting fourteen feet away from a terrorist bomb that exploded on TWA Flight 840. She appeared on *CBS Evening News with Dan Rather, 20/20, The 700 Club*, and other television and radio shows. Jeanette has been quoted in *Newsweek, The New York Times*, and *USA Today*. She's written diverse national magazine articles.

Recognized as a gifted communicator, Jeanette challenges audiences with God's life-transforming principles. She has spoken at community and church events, retreats, prisons, women's groups, schools, and hosted *Reflections*, a fifteen-minute weekly radio show that aired in cities from South Carolina to the Arctic Circle.

With her background as a multi-cultural author, educator, and missionary, she generates rapport with audiences. Her enthusiasm and warm personality sparkle in her speaking and writing style.

For over thirty-five years, Jeanette has personally interviewed some of the most inspiring and influential people of our time, gathering a fantastic collection of intimate testimonials, some of which have been included within *Extravagant Graces*. She has met with political and spiritual leaders on multiple continents.

Jeanette has lived all over the world and has visited thirty-two countries. She passionately loves adventure and missions. Her work with World Vision inspired her lifelong sponsorship of children with them.

She graduated from Westmont College, and has since earned an MA in English as a Second Language and taught at the university level.

Jeanette loves living among the lush valleys of Oregon's wine country, where she gets to be aunt to her sixteen nieces and nephews. She's entertained every day by her charming—yet sneaky—felines, Beethoven and Lady Velvet.

Jeanette with the elegant Lady Velvet.

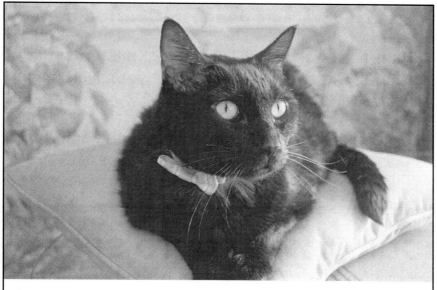

Beethoven Adorable, king of the castle.

If you enjoyed
Extravagant Graces,
please tell your friends

Things you can do to help spread the word about *Extravagant Graces*

- Write a review on **Amazon.com**

- Tweet using hashtag **#ExtravagantGraces**

- Like us: **facebook.com/Chaffee.Jeanette**

- Follow Jeanette: **twitter.com/JeanetteChaffee**

- Link to the website: **JeanetteChaffee.com**

- Share the book with your friends, pastor, church group, Bible study, book club, at your workplace, classes, and workshops

- Contact your public library and church library and ask that they carry *Extravagant Graces*

BOOK JEANETTE TO SPEAK
at your church, school, retreat, or special event:

www.JeanetteChaffee.com

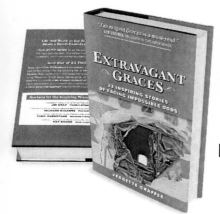

CPSIA information can be obtained at www.ICGtesting.com
Printed in the USA
BVOW07*0924120914

366343BV00001B/1/P

9 781490 829784